NORTHAMPTONSHIRE
& OXFORDSHIRE

Extracted from

AN INVENTORY OF NONCONFORMIST
CHAPELS AND MEETING-HOUSES
IN
CENTRAL ENGLAND

PREFACE

Nonconformist places of worship have for some years been the subject of detailed investigation by the Royal Commission on the Historical Monuments of England, and the records accumulated, nation-wide, will be available in the archives of the National Monuments Record. The following pages form part of the first published volume resulting from these investigations, *An Inventory of Nonconformist Chapels and Meeting-houses in Central England* (HMSO 1986). This is, however, a substantial volume, and for reasons of convenience and local interest it has also been divided into county fascicules for individual publication and separate sale, the pagination of the full *Inventory* being retained.

The subject is taken to include not only the Old Dissent of Presbyterians, Independents, Baptists and Quakers but also the New Dissent of the 18th century, the Methodists and Moravians, together with denominations of more recent origin.

Over the years denominational names have been subject to alteration: some by re-grouping, notably with the formation in 1972 of the United Reformed Church (URC); others by the more gradual process of reunion and doctrinal evolution. Original doctrinal names have, where possible, been used throughout, subsequent changes being noted in the text except in the case of Methodist groups of which only a few remained independent after 1932.

The work of investigation and recording of nonconformist places of worship, for archive and publication, has been entirely the responsibility of Mr Christopher Stell of the Commission staff. Much of it was completed before the changes in local government boundaries of 1974, and in *Inventory* and fascicules the county names and boundaries obtaining immediately prior to that date have been retained.*

---

* Accounts of the more notable nonconformist places of worship in parishes now in Oxfordshire but which at the time of recording were in Berkshire are available to the public in the Oxfordshire Sites and Monuments Record of the County Museum, Woodstock, Oxfordshire, as well as in the National Monuments Record, Royal Commission on the Historical Monuments of England.

ABBREVIATIONS

NMR   National Monuments Record
RCHM   Royal Commission on the Historical Monuments of England
URC   United Reformed Church

BIBLIOGRAPHICAL SOURCES
other than those fully titled in the text

NORTHAMPTONSHIRE AND OXFORDSHIRE

Arnold, H. Godwin 1960	'Early Meeting Houses', *Trans. Monum. Soc.*, NS VIII (1960) 89–139.
B. Hbk	*The Baptist Hand-book* (Baptist Union of Great Britain & Ireland), from 1861.
Chambers, R. F. 1963	*The Chapels of the Industrial Midlands* vol. IV of *The Strict Baptist Chapels of England* (5 vols, 1952–68).
CYB	*The Congregational Year Book* (Congregational Union of England & Wales) from 1846.
Dolbey, G. W. 1964	*The Architectural Expression of Methodism: The First Hundred Years.*
England, J. 1886–7	*The Western Group of Moravian Chapels . . . The West of England and South Wales*, in 2 parts.
Evans, G. E. 1897	*Vestiges of Protestant Dissent.*
Evans, G. E. 1899	*Midland Churches: A History of the Congregations on the Roll of the Midland Christian Union.*
Ivimey, H. 1811–30	*A History of the English Baptists*, 4 vols.
NPAB	*Proceedings and Report of the North Bucks. Association of Independent Churches and Ministers* (from 1819).
Oliver, R. W. 1968	*The Chapels of Wiltshire and the West*, vol. V of *The Strict Baptist Chapels of England* (5 vols, 1952–68).
VCH	Victoria History of the Counties of England, *Oxfordshire*, 11 vols (1907–83), in prog.
Stanley, J. *c.* 1935	*The Church in the Hop Garden* [*c.* 1935].
Summers, W. H. 1906	*The Lollards of the Chiltern Hills.*
UHST	*Transactions of the Unitarian Historical Society* (from 1917).

©Crown copyright 1986
First published 1986

ISBN 0 11 300010 3

Printed for HMSO by Acolortone Ltd   C35   6/86   Dd.736262

NORTHAMPTONSHIRE

This county, which stretches from the Cotswolds to the Fens and has ready access to important quarries of freestone and deposits of brick earth, is notable for the high proportion of early meeting-houses which have survived, one in three of those recorded being of the 18th century or before. The strength of dissent in the early 18th century manifested itself not only in the larger Presbyterian and Independent meetings principally centred on the towns, but also in many small congregations of Baptists, few of whose contemporary buildings remain. The earliest Baptist buildings, at Irthlingborough (30), of c.1723, Roade (55), of 1736–7, and Burton Latimer (12), of 1744, have all suffered from alteration or enlargement in the 19th century, an unfortunate characteristic of all the chapels in the county. Somewhat later in the 18th century are the Baptist chapels at Walgrave (66), of 1786, and Thrapston (62), of 1787, in which the contemporary use of stone and brick-work may be compared in their unaltered fronts, although they have otherwise been much changed.

Most of the early chapels which survive were built by Congregational churches although the designation Presbyterian was occasionally applied. The earliest of these is at Castle Hill, Northampton (47) where the meeting-house of 1695, notable for the ministry of Dr Philip Doddridge, is still in part distinguishable though in a greatly enlarged building. The meeting-house at Daventry (20), of 1722, is more complete in spite of refitting and minor alterations. Of the later 18th-century chapels, Kilsby (33), of 1763, and Potterspury (54), of 1780, may be especially mentioned while the former Independent chapel in West Street, Wellingborough (73), of 1791, is also of interest in having passed into Methodist use.

Of the two 18th-century Methodist chapels recorded, that at Whittlebury (78) deserves particular attention for its early date, 1763, and its associations with John Wesley. Rather earlier is the former Moravian preaching-house at Eydon (26), in use from 1751, although this was a converted building superseded in 1818. The original Moravian chapel at Woodford Halse (83), of 1798–9, is likewise remarkable in spite of later alterations.

Only two Quaker meeting-houses are listed, both in the vicinity of Wellingborough: the former meeting-house at Finedon (75), of 1690, is the earliest nonconformist building remaining in the county, while that in Wellingborough (74), of 1819, is a good example of its period. The memory of a much different denomination, the Nonjurors, remains at King's Cliffe, the home of William Law, even though the date and purpose of his 'chapel' (34) may be questioned. Other nonconformist worthies whose names are particularly associated with Northamptonshire include the Baptists William Carey, founder of the Baptist Missionary Society, and Andrew Fuller whose rebuilt chapel in Kettering (31) now bears his name, a form of distinction also adopted by Kettering Congregationalists (32) to mark the lengthy ministry of the Tollers, father and son.

Comparatively few chapels remain of interest from the early 19th century, Bugbrooke (11), of 1808, being closer in design to work of the previous century, but the gabled fronts with round-arched windows at Yardley Gobion (86), of 1826, and Charlton (45), of 1827, are typical of this period. Some later chapels, which also merit attention include a minor Gothic work by W.F. Poulton at Oundle (52), of 1864, the extraordinarily grand Classical facade at College Street, Northampton (46), of 1863, and the outstandingly original plan of High Street, Wellingborough (71), of 1875.

ABTHORPE

(1) PRIMITIVE METHODIST (SP 649464). Rebuilt 1925; reset tablet in N wall dated 1839.

ADSTONE

(2) Former WESLEYAN (SP 596516). Stone and slate. Two round-arched windows with cast-iron frames and defaced tablet dated 1849.

BILLING

(3) WESLEYAN, Great Billing (SP 811627). Opened 1836. Brick walls with rounded corners and round-arched windows.

(2) ADSTONE. Former Wesleyan chapel.

BLISWORTH

(4) BAPTIST (SP 726537). Built 1825, much rebuilt and refronted in polychrome brickwork 1871.

BRACKLEY ST PETER

(5) CONGREGATIONAL, Banbury Road, Brackley (SP 582369). Coursed rubble and slate; built in 1836 for a newly formed congregation. The front is of three bays with pilasters of a lighter

coloured stone. In the central gable is a tablet inscribed 'INDEPENDENT CHAPEL 1836'. The interior was partly refitted in the late 19th century but the original pulpit remains in the schoolroom at the rear. There are no public galleries, but above the entrance-lobby is a *singers' gallery* with staircase, seating and precentor's rostrum of *c*.1836. (URC)

Coleman (1853) 369–70.

(6) Former WESLEYAN, Brackley (SP 585371). Built 1816, superseded 1905. Coursed rubble and hipped slate roof. Gallery around three sides, rounded to rear. (Demolished *c*.1980)

BRAUNSTON

(7) WESLEYAN (SP 540661). Stone with brick dressings; gabled N front dated 1797, rendered 1875, with wide doorway, two tiers of sash windows and circular window in the gable.

The side walls have each two lower windows and one between at a higher level. The interior (32¾ft by 31¼ft) has an early 19th-century gallery around three sides with panelled front supported by timber columns and retaining contemporary box-pews; other seating is of the late 19th century. *Inscription*: on 19th-century stone tablet behind pulpit 'This chapel was erected by John and William Edmunds A.D. 1797 . . .'. *Monuments*: in chapel (1) Rev. William Breedon of Hathorn, Leics., 1837, 31 years a Wesleyan minister; in front of chapel (2) Harriet, wife of William Reeve, 1848, William their son, 1848, and Mary Ann their daughter, 1863.

BRIGSTOCK

(8) CONGREGATIONAL, School Lane (SP 946854). The congregation, which originated in the mid 18th century, was gathered into church order in 1778. Meetings were first held in a small rented building but in 1797 the church 'built a shell, the walls of stone, and covered with slate' followed by an appeal for assistance to finish the inside which was ready for use in 1798. A gallery was built *c*.1804 and in 1819 a large vestry with a school-room above was erected alongside the chapel, with shutters opening to the chapel, 'to accommodate the young and poor'. During the ministry of David Aitken (1876–85), the chapel was enlarged to the front, partly refenestrated and refitted. (URC)

The chapel has stone walls and a slate roof with half-hip to the rear. The original building (37¾ft by 28¼ft externally) has been extended to the SE (19½ft) and two tall round-arched windows in each side wall are of the date of enlargement, but the blocking of an upper window is distinguishable at the far end of the NE side. The front is gabled and has a window of three lights above the entrance. The vestry and schoolroom wing of 1819 stands against the SW side of the chapel and has a half-hipped roof. In the burial-ground to the SE are a few reset head-stones of the early 19th century and later, including some of slate. *Inscriptions*: on SW wall of chapel, square tablet with moulded cornice, inscribed in a lozenge 'Built 1797'; on SE front of schoolroom, similar tablet 'Built 1819'.

Coleman (1853) 314–26: *CYB* (1899) 160.

BRINGTON

(9) BAPTIST, Little Brington (SP 662640). Built in the early 19th

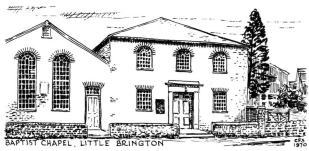

BAPTIST CHAPEL, LITTLE BRINGTON

century for a church founded in 1825. The SE front has Flemish bond brickwork with light-coloured headers and cast-iron window frames. A Sunday-school was built alongside in 1887 and the chapel enlarged in 1890.

BRIXWORTH

(10) Former WESLEYAN, Church Street (SP 747711). Brick with some coursed rubble at W end and stone quoins to older walling in front; built 1811 but altered and walls raised in 1860. Three-bay N front, original pedimented doorcase with consoles to central entrance between two heightened round-arched windows; two similar windows in gabled W wall. A stone above the N doorway is dated 1811; a tablet at the apex of the W gable is inscribed 'ENLARGED 1860'.

BUGBROOKE

(11) BAPTIST, High Street (SP 677573). Coursed rubble with ashlar W front and hipped slate roof; dated 1808. A Sunday-school wing of 1885 adjoins to the S and an organ chamber of similar date projects to the east. The interior has an original W gallery only, with panelled front; the seating and pulpit are of the

late 19th century. *Monuments*: in chapel (1) John Atterbury, surgeon, 1846, died at sea; (2) Thomas Turland, 1819, and William Brown, 1820, 'the two first deacons of this church'; (3) John Wheeler, 30 years pastor, 1835, and Jane his wife, 1831; (4) Joseph Adams, 1866, Elizabeth (Oliver) his wife, 1831, and Joseph Oliver Adams, 1823; externally on W wall (5) James Daniel, 1848.

BURTON LATIMER

(12) BAPTIST, Meeting Lane (SP 902749). The chapel, erected in 1744 for a newly-formed congregation, was extended to the rear in 1832 and altered and refitted in 1878, 1889 and later. The walls are of coursed brown ironstone and the roof is covered with stone slates. The gabled S W front originally had two doorways and windows above, all with tripartite lintels. In 1878 the doorways were replaced by a central 'Tudor' style entrance with

square label; in the blocked former doorways were set recessed bootscrapers with double scraper bars; the windows were given stone mullioned and transomed inner frames, and a shield-shaped tablet was placed in the gable recording dates of erection and alteration. The side walls have moulded stone eaves cornices and two tiers of windows, the original building being of two bays with one bay added in 1832; this date appears on a tablet on the SE wall of the extension.

The interior (originally 32ft by 30¼ft, enlarged by 14ft) has a late 19th-century boarded ceiling rising above the tie-beams of the roof trusses; there is a gallery around four sides. *Chair*: in vestry, with panelled back and two arms, believed to have belonged to Andrew Fuller, 17th-century.

Burton Latimer Baptist Church Souvenir, 1744–1944 [1944].

CLIPSTON

(13) BAPTIST (SP 709819). Brick and slate, built 1803 to replace a chapel of 1777, but with rendered pedimented front added *c*.1864. Gallery around three sides, original date-tablet of 1803 reset at foot of stairs. *Monuments*: in burial-ground, several early 19th-century slate headstones, some signed Bonsor.

CORBY

(14) Former CONGREGATIONAL, Meeting Lane (SP 896890). Small chapel of rubble with a hipped slate roof, probably dating from the mid 18th century when 'an endowed Sabbath evening lecture was commenced'; soon after 1834 the walls were heightened, a gallery inserted and the interior refitted. A hall was built 50 yards S *c*.1930 with the intention of erecting a new chapel alongside, but the project was abandoned; the former meeting-house is now used by Jehovah's Witnesses. The W front has a blocked entrance near the S end with gallery window over and a doorway and larger window to the left. There is a blocked round-arched window at the N end. The interior (42¼ft by 14¾ft) has no old features.

Coleman (1853) 332–4.

CRANFORD

(15) BAPTIST (SP 923769). Rubble with hipped roof; dated 1834.

CREATON

(16) CONGREGATIONAL, High Street (SP 707719). The congregation, originally regarded as Presbyterian, was formed in the late 17th century and a meeting-house seating 400 was erected

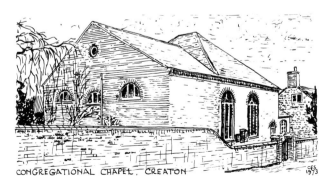

CONGREGATIONAL CHAPEL, CREATON

on a leasehold site *c*.1694. The present building, which superseded the former on the expiry of the lease, *c*.1794, has brick walls in Flemish bond with dark headers and a hipped slate roof. It was enlarged to the W in the early 19th century. The original S front had one tall round-arched window between two doorways, one of which to the W was replaced by a second window when the chapel was enlarged. The N wall has two similar windows in the older part flanking the former site of the pulpit. The gabled W wall of the extension has three upper lunettes and a single window below.

The interior (originally 35ft by 30ft, extended to W by 15ft) has a gallery in the W extension. The pulpit, re-sited on a later rostrum at the E end, is of the early 19th century; other fittings are later. *Monument*: in chapel, Rev. Joseph Whitehead, over 23 years pastor, 1816, 'such was his success as to render it necessary greatly to enlarge this place of worship'.

Coleman (1853) 179–85.

CRICK

(17) CONGREGATIONAL, Chapel Lane (SP 591724). A small chapel built soon after 1763 to replace a private room seems to have preceded the present building. The latter, of brick with a slate roof, has a gabled S front with round-arched doorway, two upper windows with wooden Y-traceried frames, all with round-arched heads, and a small tablet with moulded cornice and the date 1820. (URC)

Coleman (1823) 308–9, 313.

CULWORTH

(18) BAPTIST (SP 543470). Red brick with rendered SE front and hipped slate roof, built *c*.1842 for a church formed in that year; schoolroom wing at side added 1905. Two upper windows at front and later gabled porch. Interior refitted. (Demolished since 1971 and house built on site)

(19) Former MORAVIAN (SP 541471). The simple three-bay chapel of brick and slate with segmental-arched windows and small porch, opened 15 November 1809, has been entirely transmogrified.

England I (1886) 3, 5, pl.3.

DAVENTRY

(20) CONGREGATIONAL, Sheaf Street (SP 572624). The formerly Presbyterian congregation (now URC) which originated in the late 17th century bought a house on the NE side of Sheaf Street in 1722 and built the present meeting-house behind it which was placed in trust in July 1723. The houses, now facing the street, of three stories with brick walls and tiled roofs, were built *c*.1752; they have a three-centred arched opening leading to the rear over which a tablet placed in 1864 is inscribed 'Independent Chapel Erected A.D. 1722'. One house served as a residence for the minister, the other was used from 1752–89 by the dissenting academy formerly held in Northampton to which it subsequently returned; a tablet in the front wall records that Dr Joseph Priestley was a student here 1752–5.

The chapel has rubble walls and a hipped tiled roof originally with a central valley but altered since 1959, resulting in a raised

Exterior before late 19th-century alterations.

ridge at the front. The SW front wall, of six bays with two tiers of windows with renewed frames, was rendered in the late 19th century and the two doorways previously in the penultimate bays were re-sited in the adjacent centre bays. The rear wall, mostly covered by later buildings, had two windows flanking the pulpit, now blocked but with the timber lintels still in position, and upper windows at the ends of the galleries. The side walls are each of three bays with two tiers of windows.

The interior (41¼ft square) has two timber posts, supporting a valley-beam parallel to the front, of circular section with octagonal bases and small moulded capitals. The gallery around three sides was largely reconstructed in the late 19th century when a major refitting took place; a seating plan of 1775 indicates a single gallery at the SW end, side galleries being added *c*.1820.

Fittings – *Clock*: on front of SW gallery, octagonal face, early 18th-century. *Pulpit*: hexagonal with fielded panelled sides and staircase with twisted balusters, 18th-century, altered. *Rainwaterhead*: centrally on front wall, lead, with monogram *GR* and date 1722.

Coleman (1853) 186–209: [Thornton, A.], *1672–1972. Daventry Congregational Church, Sheaf Street, Daventry* [1972].

(21) WESLEYAN, New Street (SP 575624). Stone with rendered three-bay front, rusticated surround to central entrance between thin pilasters, platband between terminal pilasters, round-arched upper windows and pedimental gable with altered tablet dated 1824.

DESBOROUGH

(22) Former BAPTIST (SP 801835). Built *c*.1848, extended to front 1855.

EARL BARTON

(23) BAPTIST (SP 851637) Earls Barton. Gothic with gabled front, 1874 by Edward Sharman, replacing a brick meeting-house of *c*.1795. Mid 19th-century Sunday-school adjacent. *Chair*: in pulpit, with carved square-panelled back and arms supported by enriched columns, reputed to have belonged to William Carey, *c*.1700.

Exterior before 1959 alterations.

Interior from E.
(20) DAVENTRY. Congregational chapel, Sheaf Street. (URC)

ECTON

(24) BAPTIST (SP 827635). Built *c*.1829, closed 1980. Three-bay rendered front with round-arched windows and later porch. Two round-arched windows flank pulpit, one altered to doorway in 1867 when schoolroom added behind. Refitted late 19th century.

EYDON

(25) Former FRIENDS (SP 54155030). Built *c*.1701 for a meeting which in 1691 registered the house of Thomas Smallbone. It was closed in 1868 but survived as a workshop until *c*.1960; it has since been demolished.

(26) MORAVIAN (SP 542503). Preaching began in the 1740s, and about 1751 a house was purchased for use as a meeting-house. This was superseded by the present chapel which was opened 30 September 1818. The former meeting-house, at the middle of a range of buildings at one side of the courtyard in front of the chapel, is a 17th-century building, of rubble, originally of one storey and attics with a thatched roof, but since altered; the entrance was to the right of the present glazed porch beyond which was a tall window inserted when the house was converted for religious use.

The chapel, of red brick with a hipped slate roof formerly surmounted by a wooden bell-turret and weather vane bearing the Moravian emblem, was refitted in the late 19th century. The

front wall of three bays with tall round-arched windows has above the entrance a gabled bell-cote with one bell, replacing that previously on the roof. There are two segmental-arched windows in the rear wall.

Fittings – *Chandelier*: brass, 12-branch, late 18th-century. *Clock*: loose in vestry, by J. Parker, Pudsey, 19th-century.

England I (1886) pl.4.

FLORE

(27) CONGREGATIONAL, Chapel Lane (SP 646600). The present chapel, erected in 1880, stands close by its predecessor, now the

Former CONGREGATIONAL CHAPEL, FLORE

Sunday-school, built in 1810 as a preaching station for Weedon Bec with which the congregation at Flore had been associated since the late 17th century. The former chapel, of brick and slate, has a gabled W front with round-arched doorway, fanlight and semicircular canopy; two lunettes light the back of the gallery. The side and rear walls have each two tall round-arched windows. (URC)

Monuments: externally against W wall (1) Richard Clark Smith, 1822, and Mary Smith, 1843, slate headstone; (2) George Smith, 1834; other headstones of the early 19th-century stand in the burial-ground to S and west.

Coleman (1853) 266–7.

HIGHAM FERRERS

(28) WESLEYAN, High Street (SP 959683). Red brick with stone dressings, double-gabled front with elaborate pinnacles. Opened 1903.

HOLCOT

(29) WESLEYAN (SP 792698). Brick and slate, opened 1815. Two former entrances in side wall alternate with segmental-arched windows; present entrance in gable end.

IRTHLINGBOROUGH

(30) BAPTIST, Meeting Lane (SP 949708). The meeting-house was built in 1713 for a society which was reorganized as a Strict Baptist church in 1770. Galleries were added to the building in 1794. Further rooms were built at one end, the front windows were altered and the interior refitted c.1884 and other rooms

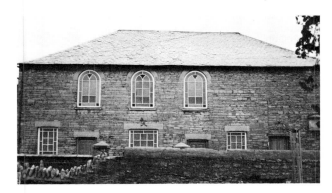

were added at the back in 1930 and 1941. The wide front has two doorways alternating with three windows, all with late 19th-century stone lintels, and three upper windows with altered round-arched heads. The rear wall has two tall round-arched pulpit windows and smaller windows at the gallery ends. The interior (28½ft by 37½ft) has a gallery around three sides; the pulpit was replaced by a rostrum c.1884.

Monuments: in chapel (1) Thomas Allen, pastor over 16 years, 1831, 'his mortal remains are deposited in the vestry'; (2) John Trimming, pastor 30 years, 1862.

Chambers (1963) 91–2.

KETTERING

(31) BAPTIST, Gold Street (SP 868789). The Baptist congregation originated in 1696 when some members separated from the Great Meeting; it is especially notable for the pastorate of Andrew Fuller (1783–1815) after whom the present chapel is named. The first meeting-house in Bayley's Yard was superseded about 1729 by the use of one in Goosepasture Lane (Meadow Road), built c.1715 for another group of Great Meeting seceders, and in 1768 by the conversion of a warehouse on the present site. The chapel was built in 1860–1 to designs by Edward Sherman of Wellingborough.

Barrett, G., *A Brief History of Fuller Church, Kettering* (1946): Chambers (1963) 88: Ivimey II (1814) 514; IV (1830) 526–34.

(32) CONGREGATIONAL, Gold Street (SP 867787). The Great Meeting was gathered in the late 17th century by John Maidwell, ejected rector of Kettering, who in 1672 took out a licence as a Congregational preacher at his own house. Meetings formerly held in a building in Allen's Yard were transferred to the present newly-erected meeting-house on Bakehouse Hill or

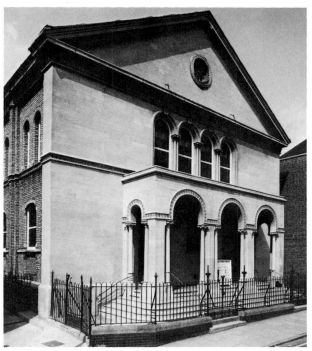

(31) KETTERING. Baptist chapel.

Newland in 1723 and the building was registered April 1724. The church experienced two notable ministries: of Thomas Northcote Toller (1777–1821), and his son Thomas Toller (1821–75), in honour of which the chapel was renamed. The meeting-house suffered from structural faults which occasioned repairs in 1728, 1741 and 1772. A major alteration and refitting was undertaken in 1849, the present front was added c.1875, and a further drastic refitting occurred in 1898–9, all of which has left little of the original structure intact.

The chapel (originally 55½ft by 48ft externally) has brown ironstone walls and a hipped slate roof; the later front is of red brick. The original side wall facing Meeting Lane, much altered but probably formerly of four bays, has two tiers of windows. The interior originally had two pillars to support the roof, replaced by four in 1741 and superseded by iron pillars in 1898–9. Among the fittings removed in 1849 was a 24-branch chandelier with dove and olive branch. A few *monuments* remain in the burial-ground at the rear, including: John Munn, 1763, slate headstone, signed G. Dawkins, Rowell. (URC)

Coleman (1853) 80–116: Goodman, F.C., *The Great Meeting* (1962).

KILSBY

(33) CONGREGATIONAL, Chapel Street (SP 562709). A dissenting congregation may have been in existence here from the late 17th century, encouraged by ejected ministers from Kilsby and Crick. In 1738 a house was fitted up for meetings and galleries added to it in 1750 and 1755. This was superseded in 1763 by the present building which has walls of squared stone and a tiled

CONGREGATIONAL CHAPEL, KILSBY

roof. The front has two doorways, windows with timber lintels and a tripartite lunette in the gable. The side walls have each two upper and two lower windows towards the back and in the rear wall are two windows, now blocked, flanking the pulpit. The interior (34ft square) has a single gallery opposite the pulpit with panelled front divided by narrow pilasters and supported by three oak columns with moulded capitals and high attic bases.

Fittings – *Monuments*: in chapel (1) Rev. Thomas Strange, 1784, pastor 1751–84, plain marble tablet inscribed '... this House erected & this Congregation greatly improved, by the blessing of God on his wise & unwearied labours, are a much nobler Monument that any which the Sculptor's art could form.'; in front of chapel (2) John son of Abraham and Sarah Lee, 1837, brick table-tomb; (3) Samuel Bartlett, 1846; (4) Rev. Horatio Ault, 20 years pastor of the United churches at Repton and Barrow on Trent, Derbys., and 14 years of this church, 1871; (5) Peter, fourth son of Rev. Horatio Ault, 1862. *Pulpit*: desk remade lower but incorporating original pulpit front; narrow backboard with inlaid sunburst and octagonal canopy with moulded cornice and ogee top surmounted by acorn finial, *c*.1763. (URC)

Coleman (1853) 304–13.

KING'S CLIFFE

(34) DR LAW'S CHAPEL (TL 007971). A building of two stories with stone walls and hipped stone slated roof, 50 yards N of Hall Farm, home of the notable non-juror Dr William Law (1686–1761), is known as 'Dr Law's Chapel' although its use as a meeting-house for a non-juring congregation is open to question. The SW wall and parts of one side wall facing the house are of ashlar; the front, of three bays with pedimented centre and round-arched entrance between similarly arched windows, has a platband and a moulded cornice of late 18th-century character. The NW wall facing the road is of rubble with altered domestic windows. The plan is irregular but the principal S corner is square. A line of glass-houses contemporary with the ashlar walling formerly adjoined on the SE side. The memory of Dr Law is also preserved at 'Library House' (TL 011970) which carries the inscription 'Books of Piety are here lent to any Persons of this or the Neighbouring Towns'.

(35) WESLEYAN, Bridge Street (TL 007971). Coursed rubble with ashlar dressings and hipped stone slated roof. Narrow three-bay front with tablet dated 1823.

KING'S SUTTON

(36) BAPTIST (SP 497363). Rebuilt *c*.1863. Stone reset in front wall inscribed 'WT 1732/WK 1733'.

KISLINGBURY

(37) BAPTIST, Mill Road (SP 695594). Squared rubble and slate; gabled front with chamfered plinth, central entrance with flat canopy between two tiers of flat-arched sash windows, and tablet in gable with moulded cornice and date 1828. Gallery at front end only. Refitted 1875.

LONG BUCKBY

(38) BAPTIST, Market Place (SP 628675). Three-bay front of squared stone, dated 1846; large gable, two tiers of round-arched windows and two doorways all with semicircular moulded labels.

(39) CONGREGATIONAL, Brington Road (SP 629674). The chapel was built in 1771 for a congregation known to have been in existence by 1709 and to have previously occupied a small meeting-house near the present site. It was enlarged to the rear in

1819, altered internally in 1859 and the fittings further modified in 1899 and 1951. The walls are of squared stone and the roof is covered with slates. The N front, of three bays surmounted by a large lunette, has a tablet inscribed 'THIS CHAPEL ERECTED 1771 R D' (for Richard Denny, pastor 1763–95). The side walls, originally of three bays with one bay added, have two tiers of windows similar to those in the front wall. The rear wall is gabled with a moulded string-course at eaves level, two widely spaced pointed-arched windows with keystones, blocked segmental-arched recesses beneath and, in the gable, a round-arched access door to the roof space below a tablet inscribed 'ENLARGED 1819'.

The interior (originally 36ft by $34\frac{1}{4}$ft, extended 14ft to S) has a gallery around three sides and a pulpit of 1859 at the S end. The 1819 enlargement provided a further S gallery behind the former site of the pulpit which was removed in 1859 but the two substantial wooden columns which supported it at each end remain below the side galleries. *Monuments* in burial ground to S include several 19th-century slate head-stones; Coleman notes a head-stone to Rev. Thomas Cartwright, 1744. (URC)

Coleman (1853) 268–74: Ivory, L.S., *Long Buckby Congregational Church, 1707–1957* (1957).

MIDDLETON CHENEY

(40) BAPTIST (SP 498418). The chapel, built in 1806 for a Particular Baptist church formed in 1740, replacing a meeting-house of 1753 in Brewhouse Lane, is a large building of coursed

ironstone rubble with a slate roof. The S front has a central doorway which replaces a pair of entrances now altered to windows; in the gable is a small tablet inscribed within a lozenge 'L 1806 May 2'. Interior refitted 1875. *Monument*: in burial-ground, to Catharine Price, 1848, and Joseph Price, 9 years minister (date obscured by concrete resetting).

MILTON MALSOR

(41) BAPTIST (SP 734555). Wide three-bay front with central doorway and small upper windows; tablet below centre window dated 1827. Front gallery added *c*.1871 and reseated 1876 but still with box-pews; rebuilt pulpit incorporates original material.

MOULTON

(42) WESLEYAN (SP 783662). Tall gabled front dated 1835; windows with intersecting wooden tracery and marginal bars. Contemporary two-storied cottages flank the chapel (one demolished since 1967).

NASEBY

(43) WESLEYAN (SP 688779). Built 1825, entirely altered 1871, Sunday-school added alongside 1903.

NETHER HEYFORD

(44) BAPTIST (SP 659584). Built *c*.1826; two segmental-arched windows in front wall with former entrance off-centre between.

NEWBOTTLE

(45) CONGREGATIONAL, Charlton (SP 527359). Dated 1827. Gabled E front of three bays with platband between two tiers of round-arched windows. (URC)

NORTHAMPTON

(46) BAPTIST, College Street (SP 753605). The church formed in 1697 erected the first meeting-house on this site in 1714; this had stone walls and two tiers of windows in three bays with two intermediate doorways, it was twice enlarged during the notable pastorate of John Collet Ryland (1759–85). The present building designed by William Hull, erected in 1863, has walls of rubble with an ashlar front. The facade, which is wider than and architecturally unrelated to the chapel behind, is an elaborate Classical composition with rusticated lower storey and a raised pedimented portico with six Corinthian columns, paired at the ends, and flanking bays with terminal pilasters. *Monuments*: re-set gravestones in paving at front and side include one to Hannah Dadford, 1787, Thomas Dadford, 1837, and Sarah Dadford.

Ivimey IV (1830) 609–10: Payne, E.A., *College Street Chapel, Northampton, 1697–1947* (1947).

Front from SW.

Interior from SE.
(47) NORTHAMPTON. Castle Hill Meeting-house. (URC)

(47) CASTLE HILL MEETING-HOUSE (SP 750606). The church meeting in Quart Pot Lane or Doddridge Street was formed in the late 17th century and initially included both Presbyterian and Independent elements, although latterly Congregational (now URC); it is notable for the ministry of Dr Philip Doddridge (pastor 1730–51) who also maintained an important dissenting academy in the town. The original meeting-house, of 1695, much altered and enlarged to the N in 1862, forms the basis of the present building which has walls of coursed ironstone rubble and a hipped slated roof. The S front of three bays is partly covered by a large vestibule built in front in 1890 but three upper windows remain with altered lintels; the lower part formerly had two doorways and two windows between. The side walls, originally of three bays with two tiers of windows, have been extended by two bays to the north. A low gabled vestry of *c*.1695 projects on the W side.

Interior of original vestry.

The interior (originally 39¼ft by 52½ft, now greatly enlarged and refitted) has side and rear galleries of 1852, extended 1862, and contemporary box-pews. Prior to 1852, when the chapel was reroofed, the roof was supported by two massive wooden pillars 'one a little bandy', and the fittings included a 'clumsy white pulpit' at the N side approached by ten steps, and 'a mighty brass branched candlestick' on a chain. The W vestry is unaltered; it has a corner fireplace and wall benches and contains a small number of historical items including the former gallery *clock* with circular face and kidney-shaped pendulum case, of the early 18th century. *Monument*: in chapel, to Philip Doddridge D.D., 1751, 21 years pastor, oval tablet with elaborate rococo surround incorporating shield-of-arms, by John Hunt and Gilbert West. *Pulpit*: now in Congregational chapel, Middleton, Wirksworth, Derbyshire (146). *Sundial*: on S wall, dated 1695.

Arnold, T. & Cooper, J.J., *The History of the Church of Doddridge* (1895): Coleman (1853) 9–37: Deacon, M., *Philip Doddridge of Northampton* (1980): Godfrey, B.S., *Castle Hill Meeting*, (1947).

(48) Former CONGREGATIONAL, King Street (SP 752606). Seceders from Castle Hill meeting who left in 1775 after a disputed ministerial appointment built a chapel in King's Head Lane in 1777; the building was considerably enlarged in 1858 and greatly extended to the W and altered in 1880; the church removed to Abingdon Avenue in 1901 and the former chapel was further altered by a variety of users. The surviving parts of the original structure, at the E end and the E half of the S wall, are of stone, with two widely spaced pointed-arched windows in the E wall and a platband above. The interior (originally about 34ft by 20ft) latterly had the pulpit at the E end. Coleman records monuments to Rev. William Hextal, 1777, and Benjamin Lloyd Edwards, 1831, 45 years pastor. (Demolished 1967)

Coleman (1853) 37–42.

(49) BAPTIST, High Street, Kingsthorpe (SP 751633). Walls of squared ironstone and slated roof. Gabled front dated 1835 with wide porch added 1892 replacing two doorways with window between; two round-arched windows above former entrances and lunette ventilator in gable. Side walls of two bays extended to rear. *Monuments*: (1) Joseph Campion, 1850, 23 years deacon, and Charlotte his widow, 1868; (2) Rev. Joseph Roberts, 1847. (Demolition proposed *c*.1976)

(50) CONGREGATIONAL, Kingsthorpe Road (SP 753619). Built 1901–3, by Alexander Anderson of Northampton. Square rising

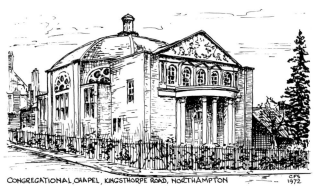

CONGREGATIONAL CHAPEL, KINGSTHORPE ROAD, NORTHAMPTON

to octagon with low polygonal dome; front pediment carved in low relief.

CYB (1903) 158–9.

NORTON

(51) WESLEYAN (SP 601638). Rubble and slate, opened 1817, possibly the conversion of an existing cottage; further altered in mid 19th century.

OUNDLE

(52) CONGREGATIONAL, West Street (TL 039881). Rubble and slate, gabled front divided into three bays by buttresses rising to plain pinnacles, two gabled porches and tall pointed-arched window of four lights with cusped tracery. Built 1864, by W.F. Poulton of Reading, superseding a meeting-house of *c*.1724.

Coleman (1853) 250–61: *CYB* (1865) 297; (1872) 410.

(53) ZION CHAPEL, West Street (TL 038881). Built in 1852 for a Particular Baptist church formed in 1800, but was latterly in Roman Catholic use. (Disused 1979)

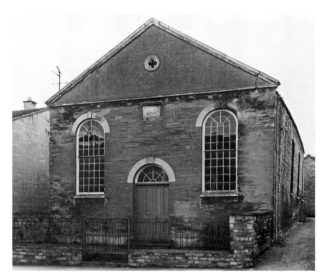

POTTERSPURY

(54) CONGREGATIONAL (SP 762434). The church (now URC) originated in the late 17th century. The chapel was built in 1780. A house for the minister was built alongside it in the same year and in 1846 Sunday-school rooms were added at the W end. The chapel has walls of brick in Flemish bond with blue headers at the front, rubble at the back and a tiled roof. The S front, which has a brick platband between two tiers of segmental-arched windows, originally had two entrances with two windows between and three above; one of the latter is dated 1780. The N wall has two round-arched windows flanking the site of the pulpit. The W extension of two stories and attics, in a similar style to the

Exterior from SW.

chapel, is dated 1846 on the keystone of the upper window in the S wall. The gabled W end has two bays of windows with lunettes to the attics.

Congregational Chapel, POTTERSPURY
Northamptonshire

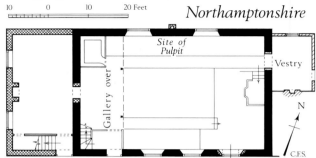

The interior of the chapel (29¼ft by 46ft) was refitted in the mid 19th century and the pulpit re-sited at the E end. The W gallery is also of the later 19th century. Fittings – *Bootscrapers*: in wall recesses, pair, with cast-iron fronts and figures of storks and bridge, mid 19th-century. *Chair*: in pulpit, oak with panelled back carved in low relief, arms with turned supports, 17th-century. *Monument*: in chapel, to Rev. Isaac Gardner, 1821, 16 years pastor. *Organ*: front with seven bays of false pipes and Gothic ornament, mid-19th century. *Pulpit*: incorporates the late 18th-century pulpit front with fluted angle panels, moulded dentil cornice and shaped back-board.

Coleman (1853) 275–90.

ROADE

(55) BAPTIST, High Street (SP 759517). The chapel was built in 1736–7 for a church formed *c*.1688; some alterations were made in the late 18th century and in 1802 a major reconstruction seems to have taken place including heightening, re-roofing and renewal of the window heads. The walls are of coursed rubble with ashlar quoins and the roof is slated. The broad N front has two doorways with a sash window between and two 19th-century windows above. Two tall sash windows in the S wall flank the pulpit, with two lower windows at either side. A two-storied vestry and schoolroom wing of the early 19th century adjoins to the west.

The interior (36¼ft by 44¼ft) has a N gallery only. The pulpit and seating date from the late 19th century. Fittings – *Baptistery*: in front of pulpit with steps at E and W ends, formerly filled by rainwater from pipe behind pulpit. *Clock*: with external face on front wall, late 19th-century. *Communion Table*: oak, with turned legs and moulded upper rails, early 18th-century. *Monuments*: in chapel (1) Mary widow of Samuel Deacon, 1796; (2) Samuel Deacon, 1779, pastor over 38 years, and Mary his daughter, 1773; (3) Rev. William Heighton, 1827, pastor nearly 40 years; (4) Rev. George Jayne, 1848, 20 years pastor.

Payne, E.A., *Roade Baptist Church, 1688–1938* (1938).

ROTHWELL

(56) CONGREGATIONAL (SP 814809) The church (now URC) was formed in 1655 and a covenant was signed by the members

in that year. The present chapel opened 9 November 1735 has been much altered and refitted, a vestry was added in 1762, in 1826 schoolrooms were built between the front entrances and in 1852 porches with gallery staircases were added, enlargements made to the rear and the roof replaced. Further works of alteration and embellishment were carried out in 1893. The walls are of coursed ironstone rubble and the roof, hipped over the original building, is covered with slates. The side walls to N and S have each three round-arched windows with keystones and three square windows above. The E front is entirely covered by the 19th-century additions which have round-arched outer doorways and paired round-arched upper windows, all of 1852; the elaborate cornice and parapet date from 1893.

The interior (40ft by 52ft) entirely refitted c.1852, has a gallery around three sides and box-pews. Prior to 1893, the projection behind the pulpit at the W end was filled with steeply raked choir seating and had a small organ against the E wall.

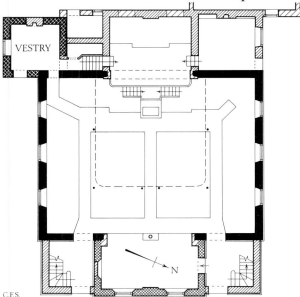

Congregational Chapel ,   ROTHWELL

10 Feet   0   10   20   30   *Northamptonshire*

C.F.S.

Inscriptions: on stone reset in N wall, date 1676; on W wall of vestry, 1762; above E front 'Restored 1893/Enlarged 1852'; reset in S wall of former stables N of chapel 'Infant School 1830'. *Panelling*: in vestry, bolection-moulded panel with inlaid decoration, incorporated in front of cupboard, perhaps from early 18th-century pulpit.

Coleman (1853) 46–79: Glass, N., *The Early History of the Independent Church at Rothwell alias Rowell in Northamptonshire* (1871): Tibbutt (1972) 61–2.

RUSHDEN

(57) Former BAPTIST, Little Street (SP 960663). The Baptist congregation in Rushden, originally part of the church meeting at Stevington, Beds., became autonomous by 1723. The meeting-house was described in 1768 as a converted tenement and seems to have stood on the present site behind other buildings. The existing structure is a rebuilding of 1796 with rubble walls and a steeply pitched hipped and tiled roof; a schoolroom and vestries were added at the back in 1860 and in 1873–4 the chapel was enlarged to the S in yellow brick with a slate roof gabled to the front. In 1901 a new chapel was opened in Park Road and the Little Street building converted for use by the Sunday-school.

E side of chapel showing N and S extensions.

The side walls have two tiers of irregularly spaced windows. The S front before enlargement had two tall doorways incorporating windows, with a window between and one above, all with flat-arched heads with keystones; between the two windows was a tablet dated 1796 now reset in the E wall. The interior (about 42ft by 32ft) had galleries around three sides and round-arched windows each side of the pulpit.

Monuments: in burial-ground to N, headstones reset around boundary walls, (1) Rev. William Knowles, 1794, 42 years pastor, slate; (2) Rev. Joseph Belsher, 1797.

Bayes, G.E., *These Years Have Told: The Story of Park Road Baptist Church, Rushden* (1951).

SHUTLANGER

(58) WESLEYAN, Twitch Hill (SP 726499). Opened 1843, altered.

SILVERSTONE

(59) WESLEYAN, High Street (SP 669439). Rubble and slate, built 1811 and extended to front c.1840. The earlier work had a broad front, gabled sides and two large segmental-arched windows in the back wall. The present front has a wide gable with a

gabled porch, two tall windows with four-centred arched heads and a shorter one above the entrance; the original date-stone of 1811 is reset in the front wall. The interior, re-pewed in the late 19th century, has a gallery of *c*.1840 at the front. *Monument*: in chapel, to George Newman Robinson, 1859.

SLAPTON

(60) WESLEYAN, Chapel Lane (SP 640468). Rubble with red brick front and slate roof. Two pointed-arched windows in front wall and tablet between dated 1844; entrance in low wing against gabled end wall, the original doorway now internal has a segmental-arched head. Gallery next to entrance *c*.1844 with coved and panelled front and contemporary open-backed benches.

SULGRAVE

(61) BAPTIST, Little Street (SP 559454). Rubble with hipped

slate roof. N front with tall sash windows and central doorway, all with tripartite lintels. Tablet over entrance dated 1844. (Becoming derelict 1971)

THRAPSTON

(62) BAPTIST, Huntingdon Road (SP 999786). The chapel, which stands back on the N side of the street, has a brick front

and rubble sides. The low roof is concealed by a rebuilt parapet. The original building of 1787 (34ft by 36¼ft externally) was extended to the N in the early 19th century. The S front is of four principal bays with a fifth bay to the W covering a side-passage. A stone tablet in the parapet is inscribed 'This place of worship/was built by public Subscription/A.D. 1787/For the Promulgation of the/Gospel of/JESUS CHRIST'.

The interior, altered in 1884–5 and later, has a gallery around three sides, box-pews, and several *wall monuments* including: (1) Robert Bateman, 1852, 'the last survivor of the little band who in 1787 united in forming the Church meeting in this place . . .'; (2) Rev. Reynold Hogg, 1843, first pastor and first treasurer of the Baptist Missionary Society; (3) Mary, widow of Thomas Ekins, 1794. In the burial-ground to the N are several slate headstones.

TOWCESTER

(63) BAPTIST, Watling Street (SP 695485). Red brick with yellow brick dressings; pedimented front with three tall arched bays enclosing two tiers of windows and central doorway. Dated 1877.

(64) CONGREGATIONAL, Meeting Yard (SP 693486). Independents formerly meeting jointly with Baptists were obliged, after 1782, to provide a separate meeting-house. The present 'Independent Chapel' built in 1845 has walls of rubble and a slate roof. The two-bay front has a brick pediment and two pedimented doorways below windows. The front and side windows are set in wide round-arched recesses with brick infilling.

Coleman (1853) 357–60.

(65) WESLEYAN, Caldecote (SP 687510). Small chapel dated 1846; of pink brick with pointed-arched windows.

WALGRAVE

(66) BAPTIST (SP 802721). The church which originated *c*.1700 was meeting by 1763 in a converted barn. The present site was acquired in 1786 and the meeting-house erected in that year. The

chapel has rubble walls and a hipped slate roof. The S front has two entrances with a three-light transomed window between and three windows above; a square stone tablet with moulded cornice is dated 1786. The N wall has two round-arched windows flanking the pulpit; a similar window in the W wall replaces the earlier fenestration. A Sunday-school of 1899 adjoins to the east.

The interior (30ft by 36½ft), drastically refitted in 1886, has a S gallery; E and W galleries have been removed.

Monuments: in chapel (1) Rev. Alexander Payne, 1819, nearly 33 years pastor, and Mary his wife, 1814, white marble oval tablet; in yard S of chapel (2) William, son of Anthony and Elizabeth Barker, 1810; (3) Elizabeth wife of Anthony Barker, 1795.

(67) STRICT BAPTIST, Zion Lane (SP 803722). Tiny, brick and slate, with two round-arched windows. Dated 1853.

Chambers (1963) 85–6.

WEEDON BEC

(68) CONGREGATIONAL, Church Street (SP 631592). The church (now URC) originated in the late 17th century and by 1688 comprised a joint congregation at Flore and Weedon Bec. The former was described *c.*1715 as Independent, but the latter was regarded as Presbyterian in 1767, in which year John Wesley, when refused the use of the Parish Church, 'accepted the offer of the Presbyterian Meeting-house'.

The present chapel, built in 1792 and registered in the following year, has rubble walls with an ashlar front and a hipped slate roof with moulded eaves cornice. The E front, which has segmental-arched doorways with altered fanlights and high pedimented canopies, is dated 1792. The side walls of two bays have two tiers of segmental-arched windows. The rear wall has two

widely-spaced semicircular-arched windows and a low brick vestry or schoolroom of 1847 projecting to the north.

The interior (42ft by 30ft) has galleries around three sides, the E gallery being the earliest and the side galleries added in the early 19th century. The windows in the N and S walls have their original wooden frames with moulded centre mullions and rectangular leaded glazing.

Fittings – Clock: on front of E gallery, early 19th-century. *Monuments*: in chapel (1) Elizabeth, wife of Rev. James Pinkerton, 1824, signed Whiting, North-ton; (2) Rev. Joseph Gronow, 1817, over 21 years pastor, Mary Catharine his wife, 1816, and their children Joseph Whitehead Gronow, 1810, and William Hodgkinson Gronow, 1818, signed 'Whiting Sculp. North-ton'; (3) John Spencer, 1808, oval tablet; in front burial-ground, two slate headstones (4) James Barge, 1822, and Ann his wife, 1821; (5) Richard Smith, 1807, and Sarah his wife, 1804; also other early 19th-century monuments (monuments in rear burial-ground have been removed or re-sited). *Pulpit*: square with fielded panels, with original pedimented back-board, all reduced in height. *Seating*: in gallery, early 19th-century; box-pews of *c.*1850 below.

Coleman (1853) 262–7.

WELDON

(69) CONGREGATIONAL, Chapel Road (SP 924897). Meetings held from 1706 in the house of Edward Nutt were transferred

CONGREGATIONAL CHAPEL, WELDON

*c.*1736–8 to a small barn on the present site, which had been converted to a meeting-house. This was replaced in 1792 by the existing chapel which was enlarged in 1808 by the addition of a gallery.

The walls are of coursed and squared limestone and the roof which is gabled to N and S is covered with stone slates. The W front has a wide round-arched window with keystone between two doorways, that to the S now blocked. There is a single upper window in the E wall and two round-arched windows at the S end. The N wall, partly covered by a lower Sunday-school wing, has a stone chimney stack at the apex of the gable.

The interior ($33\frac{1}{4}$ft by $20\frac{1}{4}$ft) has a plaster ceiling with coved sides. The single N gallery has a fielded panelled front and a wide-boarded floor; one original seat with shaped end remains next to the staircase. The pulpit and lower pews were renewed in the late 19th century.

Fittings – *Benefaction Board*: brass tablet recording the endowment in 1841 by Thomas Lash of Kettering, of a charity for distribution to the poor of Great and Little Weldon, irrespective of denomination, of 'good wheaten bread' and 'good wholesome meat' in the first weeks of November and March respectively. *Monuments*: in chapel (1) Rev. John Philip, 1837; in burial-ground (2) Rev. John Philip, 1837, Frances his widow, 1843, and Mercy their daughter 1857, table-tomb in railed enclosure; (3–5) group of three graves S of chapel, to children, including Ogden Coward, 1850, with uniform headstones, and short flat capstones covered by iron grilles.

Coleman (1853) 327–32.

WELFORD

(70) CONGREGATIONAL (SP 640803). The first permanent meeting-house for this congregation seems to have been built in 1700 on ground given by the Paynes of Sulby Hall. This was superseded in 1793 by the present chapel on a new site. The walls are

CONGREGATIONAL CHAPEL, WELFORD

of red brick and the roof is hipped and slate-covered. The NW front has a central porch replacing two doorways in the side bays; a tablet below the eaves is dated 1793. The side walls are each of two bays. Two large pointed-arched windows in the rear wall flank the pulpit. The interior (42ft by 37ft) was entirely refitted *c.*1891 and has a NW gallery of this period. *Monument*: in chapel, to Rev. Benjamin Hobson, 1848, minister 35 years.

Coleman (1853) 155–78.

Congregational Chapel   WELLINGBOROUGH, *Northamptonshire*

N

C.F.S.

Approximate Scale of Feet

0   10   20   30   40   50   60   70

WELLINGBOROUGH

(71) CONGREGATIONAL, High Street (SP 890680). The church (now URC) originated in the late 17th century, following the ejection of the vicar, Thomas Andrews, in 1662. It was originally regarded as Presbyterian. The first meeting-house in

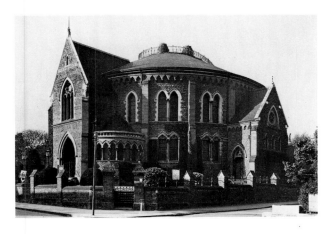

Silver Street was superseded in 1746 by a building in Cheese Lane. The present chapel was built in 1875 following the re-union in 1873 of the Cheese Lane church and that meeting at Salem Chapel (72) which had seceded from the main body in 1811.

The chapel, of coursed rubbled with a slate roof, is a notable

and unusual building designed initially by Caleb Archer, but completed under the direction of Edward Sharman of Wellingborough. The plan is ovoid with the pulpit at the narrower end and the principal entrance opposite in a gabled projection; further gabled wings at the sides accommodate the gallery stair-cases. The details are generally Gothic, with two tiers of windows at the sides and a window of three lights with cusped tracery above the main entrance.

Coleman (1853) 210–26: *CYB* (1876) 448–9: Drew, E.M., *Then and Now, a Brief History of the United Congregational Church, Wellingborough* (1925).

(72) Former CONGREGATIONAL, Salem Lane (SP 890681). 'Salem Chapel' was built in 1812 by seceders from Cheese Lane chapel, who objected to the introduction of an organ. After the reunion of the congregations, the chapel was converted for Sun-day-school use. Brick walls and hipped slate roof; much altered and refenestrated in 1875, with paired round-arched windows to the upper floor.

Coleman (1853), 246–9: Drew, *op. cit., passim.*

(73) Former CONGREGATIONAL, West Street (SP 889678). An Independent congregation formed in the late 17th century and initially part of the Rothwell church became autonomous in 1691, in which year a meeting-house was opened in Crown Yard. This was replaced in 1734 by a meeting-house in West Street which was rebuilt in its present form in 1791. The church was disbanded in 1868 and the chapel was conveyed to the Primi-tive Methodists. It is still in Methodist use.

The meeting-house is a large brick structure with ironstone plinth and a hipped roof. The wide W front, of four bays with end entrances, has a tablet dated 1791 between the upper windows. The N wall of three bays has a similar tablet dated 1734 reset from the original building. The E wall has two round-arched windows flanking the site of the pulpit.

The interior ($40\frac{1}{2}$ft by $49\frac{1}{4}$ft) has been much altered. It form-erly had a gallery around three sides, only the N gallery remains. Traces of the back-board and sounding-board of the pulpit are visible in the plaster of the E wall. A late 18th-century vestry at the S end has been enlarged.

Coleman (1853) 226–46: Drew, *op. cit., passim.*

(74) FRIENDS, St John Street (SP 889682). The meeting-house, built in 1819, has walls of squared ironstone and a hipped slated

roof. The N front has a small pedimented porch and square date-stone with moulded cornice. The interior is divided into two rooms by an entrance-passage between screens, the larger E room has a dado of reeded panelling, wall benches with shaped ends and a stand against the end wall. A stand in the W room has been removed. *Table*: in E room, dated 1667.

(75) Former FRIENDS, Church Street, Finedon (SP 919721). The meeting-house was built in 1690 on a piece of land, part of Townsend Close, which was acquired in that year. The building was much altered in the early 19th century; it was closed in 1912 and is now used as a funeral parlour. The walls are of coursed ironstone rubble and the roof, which is gabled to E and W, is slate covered. The wide S front of three bays with two segmental-arched windows and central entrance has traces of a former doorway below the W window. The N and S walls have been heightened and the outline of a steeper gable is visible at the W end.

WEST HADDON

(76) BAPTIST (SP 632719). Gabled front with two tiers of small round-arched windows. Built early 19th century for church formed 1821; refitted 1882.

WESTON AND WEEDON

(77) BAPTIST, Weston (SP 589470). The Baptist congregation in Weston existed in the early 18th century as part of a church embracing several other societies in the vicinity. The present chapel, registered July 1791 and described as 'newly erected', has walls of squared stone and a hipped slate roof. The NE front, of three bays, has a central doorway with segmental-arched bracketed canopy between tall sash windows; the windows were formerly much shorter and had segmental-arched heads. The walls appear to have been heightened in the early 19th century and a brick-fronted wing to the NW was added at that period. The interior (28ft by 22½ft), refitted in the early 19th century and later, has galleries around three sides with late 19th-century open iron fronts; the NE gallery is the earliest and has a vaulted

ceiling below. *Monuments*: in chapel (1) Thomas Kingston, 1810, and Hannah his widow, 1833, signed Cakebread, Bloxham; (2) Rev. John Law, 1805; (3) Isabel, wife of Rev. William Pain, 1807.

WHITTLEBURY

(78) METHODIST (SP 691438). On 23 June 1763 John Wesley 'preached at the side of the new preaching-house'; he visited Whittlebury on many subsequent occasions and in 1778 called it 'the flower of all our Societies in the circuit, both for zeal and simplicity'. The chapel has walls of coursed rubble and a slate

METHODIST CHAPEL, WHITTLEBURY

roof, gabled W front with central entrance and two upper windows with long timber lintels. The building of 1763 (about 25ft square externally) was enlarged to the E and the upper parts of the walls rebuilt in the early 19th century; the original thicker walling remains in the lower parts of the front and side walls and there are traces of two wide windows, now blocked, each side of the entrance.

WILBARSTON

(79) Former CONGREGATIONAL, Chapel Lane (SP 814883). An existing building fitted up for use as a meeting-house in 1793 had stone walls and a thatched roof. This was enlarged in 1820 and greatly altered in 1884 when the older part was entirely refenestrated and the roof re-covered in slates. Chapel use ceased *c*.1960. The original building (41½ft by 17ft) may have had an entrance on the W side replaced in 1884 by the present entrance in the gabled S end. An early 19th-century vestry projects at the N end of the W wall and a rendered wing on the E side may represent the work of 1820. The interior has been entirely refitted.

Monuments: in chapel (1) Rev. George Bullock, 1811, 'twenty years minister of Ashley and this place', slate tablet; (2) Frances, wife of Rev. George Bullock, 1799, elaborate slate tablet with oval inscription panel and roundel in shaped head above, with female figure and urn (see p. 154); in E wing (3) Ann, widow of Rev. George Bullock, 1826, and Ann their daughter; in burial-ground E of chapel, slate headstones including (4) Edward Ward, 1843, and Elizabeth his wife, 1823, with oval panel carved with urn and female weeper, signed 'John Bettoney, Oadby'.

Coleman (1853) 246–54.

WOLLASTON

(80) BAPTIST, Hinwick Road (SP 907626). Former chapel dated 1835. Later chapel of 1867 set back to west.

(81) Former CONGREGATIONAL, High Street (SP 908629). The chapel, standing behind houses on the E side of the street, has rubble walls heightened in brickwork. It was built in 1752 and a church was formed in 1788. The original building (30¾ft by 17¾ft) was lengthened to the S in the late 18th century incorporating a gallery and heightened in the mid 19th century. The wide W front is of three principal bays with round-arched doorway and windows and a lozenge-shaped tablet above the entrance dated 1752. The S extension has a second doorway and window above. Two windows in the N wall appear to have flanked a pulpit and a small doorway below one window leads to an early 19th-century vestry. The congregation ceased to meet in the early 20th century; the building has since been extensively damaged by fire.

Coleman (1853) 344–51.

(82) WESLEYAN, High Street (SP 907628). Coursed rubble and slate, three bay pedimented front with painted wood mouldings, tall narrow windows, central entrance with paired pilasters and entablature, and gable tablet dated 1840.

WOODFORD CUM MEMBRIS

(83) MORAVIAN, Parsons Street, Woodford Halse (SP 544526). A chapel built in 1798–9 by a newly established congregation, was altered internally and reorientated in 1828, further altered and the entrances removed to the NW end in 1875, and a new chapel built adjacent to that end in 1906.

SW wall.

The original chapel has brick walls on a stone plinth and a slate roof; it incorporates a minister's house of two stories at the SE end. The SW side of the chapel originally had two doorways with small windows above and a taller window between, replaced in 1875 by three segmental-arched windows matching similar windows in the opposite wall. The interior (23ft by 35¾ft) originally had the pulpit against the NE wall; this was removed to the SE end in 1828 when the present NW gallery was

erected. The gallery has a slightly projecting centre supported by two octagonal posts. The burial-ground behind the chapel has flat numbered tablets.

England I (1886) 4–6, pls.5–7.

WOODNEWTON

(84) WESLEYAN (TL 033944). Rubble and slate; three-bay N front with tall narrow altered windows and later porch. Tablet reset in front wall dated 1840.

WOOTTON

(85) WESLEYAN REFORM, High Street (SP 761567). Three bays with brick pilasters. Opened 1850, altered c.1900 and entrance re-sited.

YARDLEY GOBION

(86) CONGREGATIONAL (SP 766446). Rubble and slate; three-bay gabled front, two tiers of windows with semicircular brick-arched heads, lower windows partly blocked, wide arched entrance, and lunette-shaped tablet in gable inscribed 'Yardley Chapel 1826'.

Coleman (1853) 289.

YARDLEY HASTINGS

(87) CONGREGATIONAL (SP 865570). The chapel, built in 1813 to replace a meeting-house of 1718, has walls of rubble and a slate roof. The E front has an inscribed band below the pediment with

the name 'YARDLEY CHAPEL', and on a tablet between the upper windows the words 'Built 1718/Destroyed By Fire/March 1st 1813/Rebuilt and Enlarged/By Public Subscription 1813'. A late 18th-century manse adjoins to the S and a two-storied Sunday-school of the mid 19th century is against the N side.

The interior is square with the pulpit against the W wall between two round-arched windows. A gallery around three sides supported by cast-iron columns has early 19th-century pews to N and S; other seating is of the late 19th century. *Monuments*: in chapel (1) Rev. John Hoppus, 1837, 30 years pastor, and Rebekah his widow, 1843; on front wall (2) John Blower senior, son of Samuel and Mary Blower, 1832, signed 'Bunyan, Newport'. (URC)

Coleman (1853) 291–303.

YARWELL

(88) WESLEYAN (TL 069979). Built 1840, with cottage and Sunday-school added at S end. The chapel originally had two doorways in the W wall now altered to windows. The present S entrance is approached through a passage behind the cottage, in which is a separate doorway leading to a deep S gallery. The interior has been refitted.

YELVERTOFT

(89) CONGREGATIONAL (SP 598754). This congregation originated in the early 18th century when the minister from Welford registered a house for mid-week preaching. In 1758 a barn was fitted up for a meeting-house and the present chapel was erected in 1792; it was enlarged to the front in 1832 and schoolrooms built in the mid 19th century.

The chapel (originally 34½ft by 29½ft externally) has brick walls and a slated roof hipped to the rear. The gabled N front, of 1832, is of three bays with a later porch between round-arched windows and a circular window above between a pair of lunettes. In the W wall are two round-arched windows of 1792. *Monument*: N of chapel, to Jane, widow of Rev. Henry Knight, later wife of Thomas Broughton, 1847.

Coleman (1853) 335–42.

(79) WILBARSTON. Former Congregational chapel. Slate tablet.

Early nonconformity in Oxfordshire is more apparent in the development of congregations of Baptists and Quakers than in those of the Presbyterians and Independents. Friends' meeting-houses were particularly numerous and of those that survive West Adderbury (106), of 1675, is especially notable and is one of the oldest in the country. A very similar building of 1692 exists at South Newington (94) and another at a smaller scale in Burford (23), of 1709. The larger meeting-house at Banbury (11), of 1751, has been greatly altered but that at Charlbury (26), of 1779, remains with little appearance of change. The late 19th-century Friends' meeting-house at Sibford Gower (92) is of interest as one of the few rebuilt to a larger size at a time when the society generally was suffering from a period of decline.

The Baptist chapel at Cote (6), of c.1739, may be claimed to be the most picturesquely sited of all the buildings listed in the county and as such is relatively well known. Although refitted in 1859 the continued use of box-pews and the rare presence of a table pew add to its significance. The chapel at Hook Norton (57), rebuilt in 1787, is also of some interest, but other Baptist chapels are relatively small or late. The early 19th-century refronting of New Road, Oxford (76) is a not entirely successful attempt to introduce architectural embellishment and the simple detailing and good proportions of the village chapels at Chadlington (25) and Leafield (65) may generally be preferred.

Although Presbyterian congregations existed in the major towns in the early 18th century most suffered a decline prior to more or less drastic reformation as Congregational churches. Only at Banbury (8) did Unitarianism develop in any strength, and to a lesser degree in the shorter-lived village churches of Bloxham and Milton (18, 69) at the first of which the meeting-house still remains intact. The only surviving town meeting-houses of the early 18th century are at Bicester (15), where the original external appearance can still be distinguished though the interior has been greatly altered, and at Witney (111) where it has outlasted its successor, but neither building is now in use for worship.

The development of the Gothic style in chapels is evident in the early 19th century, the Congregational chapel at Witney (112), of 1828, being an outstanding example and its demolition a major loss to nonconformist architecture. The chapel of the same denomination at Binfield Heath (46), of 1835, is one of several in the vicinity of Reading incorporating a tower on a much reduced scale. Later 19th-century Gothic chapels are typified by the Baptist chapel at Chipping Norton (31), of 1863, and W.F. Poulton's Congregational chapel at Thame (102), of 1871, while the castellated architecture of the Salvation Army was ably represented by the Oxford citadel (80) of 1888.

Methodism, born in the Holy Club at Oxford, has left many small chapels of which Freeland (51), dated 1805, and Watlington (104), of 1812, may be cited as examples; few larger buildings were required outside Oxford itself where the progression from small preaching-house (78) to Classical temple and on to large Gothic chapel is still partly visible in the same street. The transformation of an early 18th-century mansion in Burford (24) is also remarkable for the outward respect paid to an important example of domestic architecture.

The presence of good building stone in the county and of stone slates, notably from the vicinity of Stonesfield, has resulted in a predominance of these materials. Brickwork appears in the early 18th century at Bicester (15) for the front wall of the meeting-house and, at the end of the century, at Goring (52), as well as in several small 19th-century chapels in districts where stone was less freely available. The incursion of slate and, less frequently, tile as a replacement for other roof coverings is general, but thatch still survives on former chapels at Bloxham (18), Dorchester (40) and Epwell (44).

ALVESCOT

(1) STRICT BAPTIST (SP 271046). Rubble and slate, built early 19th century for church formed 1833. Gabled ends; doorway in side wall with stone brackets and moulded hood. Rear gallery with original open-backed pews, other seating replaced.

Monument: in burial-ground, Charlot (sic), daughter of John and Levina Peyman, 1840, headstone with urn in low relief.

(2) Former PRIMITIVE METHODIST (SP 270047). Built 1850, converted to reading-room 1885, now used as scout hut.

ARNCOTT

(3) WESLEYAN, Green Lane (SP 610174). Rubble with hipped slate roof, two tiers of windows in front with timber lintels and slightly altered tablet between lower pair originally inscribed 'W.C./1834'. Interior refitted.

ASCOTT-UNDER-WYCHWOOD

(4) BAPTIST, Shipton Road (SP 300187), behind 'The Swan' p.h. Long low outbuilding of rubble, converted c.1816.

ASTON BAMPTON AND SHIFFORD

(5) BAPTIST, Aston (SP 340031). Coursed rubble walls and slate roof, three-bay front with pointed-arched openings with thin labels and tablet over entrance. 'BAPTIST/CHAPEL/1845'. Two pointed-arched windows in each gabled end wall.

(6) BAPTIST, Cote (SP 351031). The Baptist church now meeting at Cote was formed in 1656 by division from the Abingdon church and originally met at Longworth, Berks, 3½ miles south-east. The site of the present chapel was acquired 1703–4 and the first meeting-house registered 22 September 1704. From a mortgage dated 26 February 1739/40 it appears that the chapel was then enlarged or rebuilt to its present size, the capacity being increased in 1756 by the addition of a gallery. Drastic internal alterations were carried out in 1859 in which the pulpit was removed from the S to the W wall, the galleries altered or rebuilt against the other three walls and the seating renewed.

The chapel has stone walls and a double roof covered by stone slates. The E front has a truncated gable, formed by a screen wall across one end of the central valley, surmounted by a stone panel with scrolled ends, an alteration possibly dating from the early 19th century. Two entrances have fielded panelled doors and flat canopies with shaped timber brackets. The W wall also has a screen wall across the end of the valley, two round-arched upper windows and a central window, now blocked, below. Two tall windows in the S wall flank the former site of the pulpit. A vestry against the N wall has been enlarged.

The interior (34ft square) has galleries around three sides with staircases in the NE and SE corners, the former incorporating work of the mid 18th century. The seating, entirely of 1859, comprises box-pews with a central table-pew above the baptistery. Some earlier panelling is re-used against the W wall and as a screen in the vestry.

Fittings – *Monuments*: in chapel, on S wall (1) Mary widow of John Williams, 1837, signed Godfrey, Abingdon; (2) Martha and Mary, twin daughters of William Talbot and Abigail Wallis, 1835, and Elizabeth Stewart Wallis, 1848; on W wall (3) Rev. Thomas Sunscombe M.A., 26 years pastor, 1811; in burial-ground many 18th-century headstones with elaborate carving, including (4) Francis Taylor, 1713, cherub's head with scrolls and egg-and-dart border; and (5) Mary, wife of John Williams, 1774, scrolled border ornamented with roses and urn, background formerly coloured black. *Plate*: includes a two-handled cup of 1734, given by John Morse 1774.

Stanley [c.1935].

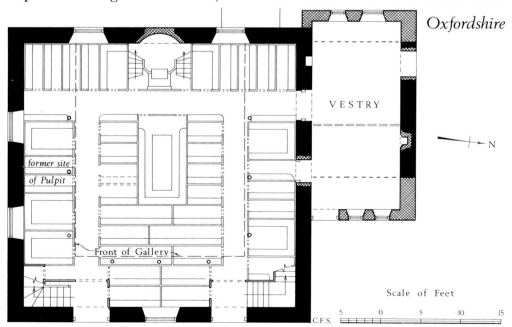

Baptist Meeting-house at Cote, ASTON BAMPTON AND SHIFFORD

Oxfordshire

VESTRY

N

former site of Pulpit

Front of Gallery

Scale of Feet

5   0   5   10   15

C.F.S.

Exterior from SE.

Interior from SE.
(6) ASTON BAMPTON AND SHIFFORD. Baptist chapel, Cote.

BAMPTON

(7) BAPTIST (SP 316032). A Quarter Sessions certificate of October 1778 probably relates to this building which was erected for the use of the minister of Cote chapel. The walls are of coursed rubble and the roof is hipped and covered with stone slates. The E front of three bays has a segmental-arched doorway formerly with a pedimented canopy, a small window above and two plain round-arched windows each side; there are two similar windows in the S and W walls. The interior (32ft by 24ft) has an E gallery with panelled front and original seating; the lower pews have been renewed and the late 18th-century pulpit at the W end has been reset lower. (Lower pews reported 1981 to be replaced by chairs)

BANBURY

(8) Site of OLD MEETING-HOUSE, Horsefair (SP 453405). The site was acquired in 1716 by a Presbyterian, latterly Unitarian, congregation which converted an existing building into a meeting-house, altered or rebuilt it c.1742 and in 1850 replaced it by a Gothic chapel. This last was succeeded c.1965 by a Baptist chapel (see (9) below). Reset in boundary wall, foliated gable-cross from 1850 chapel.

Evans (1897) 9: *UHST* I (1917–19) 276–302.

(9) Former BAPTIST, Bridge Street (SP 458406). The chapel, built in 1841, was greatly altered in 1903 to designs by A.E. Allen; a more drastic change c.1975 on conversion to a supermarket followed the removal of the congregation to the Horsefair (8).

Front before conversion.

The original front was of two bays with a pediment supported by three pairs of Ionic columns and entrances in flanking wings. In 1903 the two middle columns were re-sited to support a narrower pediment slightly in advance of its predecessor and a central entrance was constructed. Only the columns and their superstructure now remain.

B. Hbk (1902) 346; (1905) 443–4: Potts, W., *Banbury Through a Hundred Years* (1942) 75.

(10) CONGREGATIONAL, South Bar Street (SP 454404). The congregation formed in 1787 built a meeting-house in 1790 in Church Passage which, after the erection of the present building in 1857, survived in other uses until after 1942 but has since been demolished. The present chapel, on a site partly concealed by earlier buildings, is by W.M. Eyles of London. It has stone walls with a front of three bays, the centre projects and has tall pilasters supporting a Doric entablature. The entrances, in flanking wings, have Doric columns *in antis* and windows over. (URC)

(11) FRIENDS, Horsefair (SP 454406). The site was acquired in 1664 and a meeting-house erected in 1664–5 which was largely rebuilt in 1748–51 although retaining parts of the N wall and one end wall. This was drastically reconstructed in 1861 and the present building retains little earlier work beyond the basic

structure of walls and roof. The walls are of stone and the roof hipped and covered with stone slates. The S front has been refenestrated and the entrance is now at the W end. The interior (43¾ft by 21¼ft) had galleries on E, S and W sides of which only the last remains. The stand now at the E end but perhaps formerly on the N wall has also been renewed.

(12) Former WESLEYAN, Church Lane (SP 456406). Pedimented front with paired pilasters. Built 1812, enlarged 1828, sold 1865 to Primitive Methodists, now in commercial use.

BARFORD ST JOHN AND ST MICHAEL

(13) Former BAPTIST, Barford St Michael (SP 436328). Dated 1838.

(14) WESLEYAN, Barford St Michael (SP 436325). Dated 1840, with initials 'W.N.' on keystone of front window. Kelly (1931) calls this 'Reformed Wesleyan'.

BICESTER

(15) CONGREGATIONAL, Chapel Street (SP 585223). The congregation, originally Presbyterian, was gathered after 1662 by John Troughton, fellow of St John's College, Oxford. In 1672 Troughton's house was registered as a meeting-place and in October 1691 a certificate was issued for the 'New house of Henry Cornish'. The latter was superseded in January 1728 by the present building, then described as in Water Lane adjoining the Swan Inn.

The walls are of rubble with a front of brick on a rubble plinth

and the roof is hipped and slated with a central valley. The W front, of five bays, greatly altered about 1873, formerly had a central entrance above which was a circular window beneath a gablet, flanked by tall round-arched windows. Two similar windows in the E wall adjoin the original site of the pulpit.

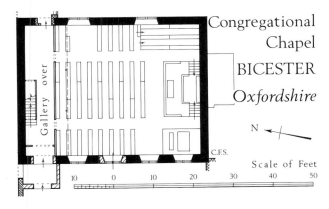

Congregational Chapel BICESTER Oxfordshire

N ←

C.F.S.

Scale of Feet
10   0   10   20   30   40   50

The interior (33½ft by 44ft), also reconstructed, now has a rostrum pulpit at the S end and a single gallery opposite supported by two turned wood columns of the 18th century. The original roof structure survives and closely resembles that at Buckingham, Bucks. (16). (Chapel closed; under conversion to recreational use 1982)

Fittings – *Clock*: on E wall, Parliament clock with arched dial

and chinoiserie decoration on case, signed 'George Langford, London', early 18th-century. *Monuments*: in chapel on E wall (1) Thomas Sirrett, 1828, and his wives, Mary, 1797, and Sarah, 1827; (2) John son of Thomas and Sarah Sirrett, 1849; on S wall (3) Rev. Richard Fletcher, 36 years pastor, 1832, his wives Mary, 1810, and Ann, 1812, and his daughters Mary, 1815, and Hannah, 1820, signed Godfrey, Abingdon; (4) William Rolls, 1798, and Mary his widow, 1803, with later inscriptions to John, father of William Rolls, 1733, Elizabeth his wife, 1777, and Elizabeth wife of Thomas Harris, daughter of William and Mary Rolls, 1799, marble tablet with shaped apron and surmounted by urn in low relief against obelisk-shaped backing; on W wall (5) Samuel Sayer, Gent., 1778, and Benjamin Sayer, 1781, 'The Grandchildren of The Learned and Revd John Troughton M.A. & Fellow of St John's College Oxford from whence he was Ejected for Nonconformity 1662', grey marble tablet; (6) James Gurden, 50 years deacon, 1830, Susannah his wife, 1810, 'by whom he had 14 children', and Benjamin their youngest son, 1808; externally, E of chapel, loose (7) Ann, wife of Andrew Major, Apothecary and Surgeon, daughter of William and Elizabeth Wheeler, 1729.

(16) Former WESLEYAN, North Street (SP 584228). Built 1841, now the Masonic Hall. Rubble with rendered dressings; pedimented front concealed by extension over forecourt 1976.

BLACKTHORN

(17) CONGREGATIONAL (SP 621193). Coursed rubble and slate. Front resembles Launton (64) but with lintel to central entrance

CONGREGATIONAL CHAPEL, BLACKTHORN

and without parapet finials; seating of loose benches with panelled backs and shaped arm-rests also comparable. Said to have been built 1841 but stylistically slightly later. At rear is part of a late 18th-century building of two stories comprising a former cottage and minor rooms now used for church purposes. (URC)

BLOXHAM

(18) Former PRESBYTERIAN (SP 430357). The 'Court House' immediately S of the Parish Church, of stone with a thatched roof, incorporates part of a building of 1610 and some earlier details. The building largely dates from the late 17th century and

(24) BURFORD AND UPTON AND SIGNET. Wesleyan chapel, High Street, Burford.

was used until *c.*1842 as a Presbyterian meeting-house by a congregation which existed jointly with a society of slightly earlier origin meeting in Milton.

Evans (1899) 77–8: *UHST* II, pt2 (1920) 9–32.

BODICOTE

(19) WESLEYAN (SP 460377). N front gabled with terminal pilasters, dated 1845.

BOURTON

(20) WESLEYAN, Little Bourton (SP 458441). Brick and slate. Gabled front dated 1845.

BRIZE NORTON

(21) PRIMITIVE METHODIST (SP 299080). Although dated 1908, this chapel appears to be of *c.*1840 and may perhaps be the former Congregational chapel built in that year. The walls are of rubble and the roof slated. Gabled front with round-arched entrance.

BURFORD AND UPTON AND SIGNET

(22) BAPTIST, Witney Street, Burford (SP 254121). The congregation which originated *c.*1700 built the present meeting-house in 1804 on the site of its predecessor. It has stone walls and a slated roof. The gabled front has a central doorway with flat hood and shaped stone brackets, two round-arched windows to the lower stage and one above. Interior, much altered in 1886 and later, has a rear gallery with front incorporating re-used

fielded panels. *Monuments*: in chapel (1) Rev. John Smith, pastor, 1807; (2) John Waymouth of Exeter, who died in Burford 18 May 1768 'when on a journey to Bristol for the recovery of his health'. *Singers' Desk*, with splayed top, early 19th-century.

(23) FRIENDS, Pytts Lane, Burford (SP 252121). The meeting-house built in 1709 superseded one at Barrington, 2 miles west. It was closed in 1854, reopened for twenty years at the beginning of the 20th century and again reopened in 1955. The walls are of stone and the half-hipped roof is covered with stone slates. The N front is of three bays. A window in the E wall has been

Friends' Meeting-house, BURFORD & UPTON & SIGNET

Oxfordshire

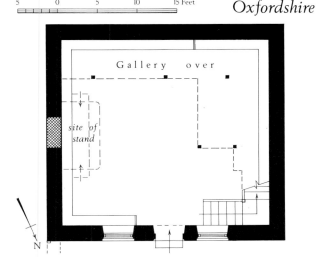

blocked; a corresponding window in the W wall comes at gallery level. The interior (26ft by 24ft) has a gallery along the S and W sides with signs of enlargement, and an attic room above lit by windows inserted in the end walls in the later 18th century. The lower walls are lined with a dado of horizontal boarding rising on the E side at the back of the former stand removed 1947.

(24) WESLEYAN, High Street, Burford (SP 252122). Large baroque mansion house of c.1715, former residence of the Chapman family, sold in 1848 and converted to a chapel in 1849 by removal of the upper floor and partitions. The elaborate ashlar front has a giant order of Corinthian pilasters with full entablature and balustraded parapet. Stone urns formerly on the parapet and flanking the stairs to the entrance were removed in 1849 to Cornbury Park, Oxfordshire.

Burford Methodist Church Centenary, 1849–1949 [1949].

CHADLINGTON

(25) BAPTIST (SP 330219). Dated 1840. Coursed rubble with ashlar dressings and hipped slate roof.

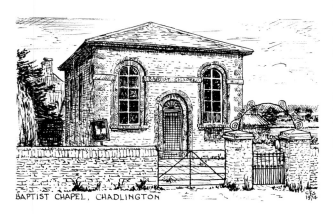

BAPTIST CHAPEL, CHADLINGTON

CHARLBURY

(26) Former FRIENDS, Market Street (SP 357196). A meeting-house of 1681 was superseded by the present building in 1779.

Coursed rubble with hipped slate roof. Broad S front with three round-arched windows with red brick surrounds and stone cills. Wide doorway left of centre and small stone tablet above with date of erection. Later lean-to extension to west. Interior (approx. 39ft by 20½ft) is divided into two rooms by an original screen. Now an architect's office.

(27) WESLEYAN, Fisher's Lane (SP 359194). Built 1823, Sunday-school adjacent 1844. Gabled front of three bays with two tiers of round-arched windows with intersecting glazing bars.

CHARLTON-ON-OTMOOR

(28) BAPTIST (SP 560156). Low rubble walls and hipped slate roof. Built c.1843 for a church formed in that year. *Pulpit*: elaborate Gothic backboard of five bays with crocketed ogee-headed side panels behind later rostrum pulpit.

CHINNOR

(29) CONGREGATIONAL (SP 756013). The chapel has walls of flint with brick dressings, rendered to the SW, and a hipped slated roof. It was built in 1805 but considerably enlarged in 1811; alterations of the late 19th century, in 1862–8 and 1888, included heightening and re-roofing and renewal of the pews. The original entrance is in the NE wall with two round-arched windows above, traces of a former gable and of a slight enlargement to each side. Two windows in the SE wall flank the pulpit, reset between them is a lozenge-shaped tablet 'erected 1805'. A new entrance was made on the SW side in the later 19th century.

The interior, which is nearly square, has a gallery of c.1811 around three sides with a blind balustraded front ornamented at the corners by flat obelisks. Some early 19th-century benches with shaped ends remain at the back of the NW and SW galleries. *Monument* in burial-ground to SW, 'The Venerable Father Mead', born 1747, died 1843, who in 1762 'was converted in this village under a sermon by the Revd. George Whitefield.'

Summers (1905) 225–8.

(30) Former INDEPENDENT (SP 756011). A brief secession from the Congregational chapel (29) resulted in the building of a second chapel opened 26 June 1826 and placed in trust 19 September 1826. The congregations reunited c.1828. The former chapel, now the Congregational manse, has rendered walls and a tiled roof, half-hipped at one end. Front of three bays with central entrance and added dormers.

CHIPPING NORTON

(31) BAPTIST, New Street (SP 312272). Built 1863, by Gibbs, Thomson and Colbourne, for church formed 1694. Drastic internal alteration 1980.

(32) Former FRIENDS, New Street (SP 311271). Stone with hipped slate roof, built 1804 superseding a building of 1695. Closed 1910; much altered 1975 on conversion to two cottages. Original round-arched entrances remain in N and E walls.

(33) Former WESLEYAN, Distons Lane (SP 312272). A chapel now converted to two houses, standing immediately behind the Baptist Chapel, was built in 1796 and superseded by the present chapel in West Street in 1868. Coursed rubble and slate with wide gabled S front with central doorway and two tiers of windows, all altered or inserted. Side walls originally of two bays partly covered on the W by a low annexe but with two upper

windows remaining on this side and small square tablet between inscribed with the date of erection.

CLANFIELD

(34) Former PRIMITIVE METHODIST (SP 287021). Gabled front to N with outline of former pointed-arched doorway. Traces of flanking windows and defaced tablet above. Built 1844, much altered on conversion to cottage 'Greenfield'.

CLAYDON WITH CLATTERCOT

(35) Former PRIMITIVE METHODIST, Claydon (SP 456500). Brick and slate; built 1837, rebuilt 1861.

CROPREDY

(36) WESLEYAN (SP 469468). Dated 1881. A former chapel of 1822 stood behind, where a house of red brick may incorporate parts of the earlier building.

DEDDINGTON

(37) Former CONGREGATIONAL, The Tchure (SP 467316). A 'dissenting congregation of great antiquity' is reported to have decayed following the introduction of heterodox preaching and the meeting-house closed. A fresh attempt to commence services was made about 1819 under the auspices of the North Bucks. Association of Independent Churches and a Mr Harris converted a barn for their use which was opened in August 1820. The new cause developed into a Congregational Church, formed 1842, and continued to use the barn until the present chapel in New Street was built in 1881 to the designs of John Sulman.

The former barn stands on the S side of a lane opening from the E side of New Street and is now named the 'Foresters Hall'. It has coursed rubble walls and a slate roof. The N front has a small doorway remaining from its earlier use blocked and superseded in 1820 by end entrances with windows over and two windows between. The S side, presumably facing the former farmyard, has traces of a wider barn opening near the W end together with a later doorway and windows.

CYB (1879) 409: *NPAB* (1820) 17–9; (1821) 14–15.

(38) WESLEYAN REFORM, Chapel Square (SP 468316). Brick and slate with square rendered front, central round-arched doorway between pair of two-light windows and wider window of three lights above. Tablet over entrance dated 1851 and a gallery inside of this period but otherwise largely refitted in late 19th century.

Former Chapel at rear, facing Church Street, of coursed rubble with a hipped slate roof was built in the early 19th century but altered c.1851 when a gable with urn finials was added to the E front incorporating a tablet inscribed 'WESLEYAN SUNDAY SCHOOL 1822'. The front has a narrow doorway between a pair of windows, all with lintels and keystones. Two windows in the S wall have timber lintels. A round-arched recess remains internally at the W end marking the site of the pulpit; a fireplace in the N wall was probably added on conversion for Sunday-school use.

(39) Former CONGREGATIONAL, Hempton (SP 446318). Built c.1849. Now in farm use.

DORCHESTER

(40) Former BAPTIST, Watling Lane (SU 576943). Small cob and thatch building attached to and now forming part of an earlier timber-framed cottage 'Orchard House' was registered for worship in 1820. The Baptist church formed in 1849 which was in membership with the Berkshire Association was dissolved before 1882. The chapel, possibly a pre-existing structure, was slightly extended to the N in brickwork in the early 19th century and given an entrance in the N wall to which a small porch was later added.

(41) Former PRIMITIVE METHODIST, Bridge End (SU 579938). Low building with rendered walls. Built c.1839; later used by Salvation Army and now converted to a cottage.

EAST ADDERBURY

(42) Former WESLEYAN (SP 471356). Ironstone with two round-arched windows in N wall flanking site of pulpit. Roof lowered. Built 1810; superseded by present chapel 150 yards W in 1893.

ENSTONE

(43) WESLEYAN, Neat Enstone (SP 377244). Brick and slate with two wide round-arched windows in front and back walls. Lower extension at SW end. Opened 1811 incorporating some older masonry in rear wall.

EPWELL

(44) Former CHAPEL (SP 353405), immediately NE of the parish church. Coursed stone walls and a thatched roof, appears to have been registered in 1825 for a ' Revivalish', possibly Baptist, meeting. It soon after passed to (Primitive) Methodists who used

it until c.1970; it is now used for storage. The S front has two sash windows, possibly alterations, and an inserted doorway to the left. In the W end is a former doorway with window above, both now blocked.

EWELME

(45) Former WESLEYAN (SU 644916). Brick with three-bay gabled front and two tiers of windows; dated 1826. Now a post office.

EYE AND DUNSDEN

(46) CONGREGATIONAL, Binfield Heath (SU 744779). Diminutive Gothic chapel of ashlar with a slated roof, built 1835 under the influence of Rev. James Sherman of Reading. Narrow battle-

mented tower at NW end incorporating porch with arched entrance and ogee label with finial. Side walls of five bays with two-stage buttresses and lancets. Sunday-school to SE added 1836.

Summers (1905) 189–90.

EYNSHAM

(47) BAPTIST (SP 431092). Rubble and slate, gabled front with parapet and small finial, three bays with four-centred arched doorway and square moulded labels. Tablet between windows 'erected A.D. 1818'. *Monuments*: in front of chapel (1) Nathaniel E. Adams, 1835; (2) Frances wife of Richard Buckingham, 1837.

FENCOTT AND MURCOTT

(48) PRIMITIVE METHODIST, Murcott (SP 589154). Gabled front with small circular window above a recent porch. Stone tablet at apex of gable dated 1847.

FILKINS AND BROUGHTON POGGS

(49) PRIMITIVE METHODIST, Filkins (SP 237042). Dated 1853. With wide pointed-arched windows.

FINSTOCK

(50) WESLEYAN (SP 361161). Built 1840, school extension in front 1902.

FREELAND

(51) WESLEYAN (SP 415127). Rubble with half-hipped roof covered with stone slates. Original front to SE has blocked

round-arched doorway between windows and small circular recess above which is a painted metal panel 'NOV 19th/ WESLEY'S/CHAPEL/1805'. Later doorway added at SW end.

GORING

(52) COUNTESS OF HUNTINGDON'S CONNEXION (SU 599807). An Independent church was formed in 1786, the members subscribing to a Confession of Faith 64 pages in length and divided into 33 chapters. The first meeting-house on the present site was built in 1793 and opened by Lady Ann Erskine, it was superseded in 1893 but survives in altered form as the Sunday-school. This has walls of brick with some flint at the sides and a hipped and tiled roof with a central flat or valley. The N front is of three bays with two tiers of windows and a central arched entrance all with late 19th-century dressings. The S wall has two original round-arched windows flanking the site of the pulpit. The interior (25¼ft by 27½ft) has a gallery around three sides with panelled front divided by fluted pilasters and supported by square wooden posts; some original seating remains in the gallery. (Entirely refitted c.1980)

Summers (1905) 107–10.

GREAT HASELEY

(53) Former CONGREGATIONAL (SP 641019). Built c.1841.

GREAT MILTON

(54) WESLEYAN (SP 629030). Rubble with brick dressings and tiled roof; three-bay gabled front with lancet windows, pointed-arched doorway in later porch, and tablet dated 1842.

HENLEY-ON-THAMES

(55) Former INDEPENDENT, New Street (SU 762829). Now 'Kenton Theatre', was built 1809 for a section of the older Congregational church which seceded in that year but ceased to meet after 1836. It stands behind other buildings on the N side of the street and has brick walls with two round-arched windows to each side.

Summers (1905) 120.

(56) FRIENDS, Northfield End (SU 759831). Part of an existing range of buildings was in use as a meeting-house from c. 1668 and purchased in 1672. This was demolished and the present meet-

ing-house of brick and tile with terracotta dressings built on the site in 1894. An early 17th-century timber-framed cottage which formed the end bay of the range adjoins to the south-east.

HOOK NORTON

(57) BAPTIST, High Street (SP 354331). The chapel, built in 1787, replaces one of 1718. It has walls of ironstone and a hipped roof now re-covered in tiles. Two round-arched windows in the N wall with later cast-iron intersecting glazing bars are repeated on the S and E sides. The entrance is at the W end in a two-storied porch which incorporates the gallery staircase; there are four

small windows at two levels in the W wall. Between the N windows is a stone tablet reset from the previous chapel with the initials and date H/WA/1718 (see monument 3 below).

The interior (36¾ft by 26¼ft) has an original W gallery with fielded panelled front, and later galleries added along the N and S walls. The box-pews and pulpit, which date from a re-fitting of 1856, have stop-chamfered panelled sides. The roof is supported by two king-post trusses and butt-purlins.

Fittings – *Monuments* and *Floorslab*. Monuments: on N wall (1) James Walford, 1840, and Mary his widow, 1846, oval stone; (2) Ann Poole, 1817, oval stone; (3) William Harwood of Broad Marston, Glos., 1720/1, 'of his piety towards God & Benevolence to Mankind This Edifice for Divine Worship And other Donations at this Place of his Nativity are Perpetuated as a Memorial . . .', also his niece Elizabeth Griffith, 1721, and his widow Anne, daughter of Thomas Edwards of Rhual, Flints., n.d., marble tablet with moulded base and capping; on E wall (4) James Wilmot, 1795, Ruth his wife, 1795, and James their son, 1799; (5) Charles Newberry, 1820, and Patience his widow, 1833; on S wall (6) George Westbury, late of Wigginton, 1728, recording that he added £40 to a gift of £20 from Amos Sansbury of Banbury 'to purchase a burying place at Hooknorton' and that he 'bought Bury Orchard for that Purpose, where he lieth interr'd', later inscription below 'This Meeting House Rebuilt 1787'; (7) Mary, wife of James Surridge, 'Citizen & Freeman of the Clock-makers Company, London', 1790, and two infant sons. *Floorslab*: re-used as threshold to W door, worn, with date 1765.

The burial-ground N of chapel contains many 18th-century headstones, some carved in high relief with cherubs heads and decorative cartouches.

Ivimey II (1814) 517–21.

(58) FRIENDS, Southrop (SP 357328). The meeting-house built in 1704 which stood SE of Southrop House was demolished in 1950. It had stone walls and a gabled roof covered with stone slates, two timber mullioned and transomed windows and a doorway in the SE side and a third window in the SW gable wall. The interior (28½ft by 16ft) had a stand at the SW end and a small gallery opposite. A rubble boundary wall remains around the site.

Drawings and photographs by H. Godwin Arnold in NMR.

HORLEY

(59) WESLEYAN (SP 418436). 'A building lately erected at Horley' registered in March 1802 was probaby the rear portion of the present chapel, built as an extension to a 17th-century cottage and enlarged to the front c.1840. The chapel has walls of ironstone rubble with a gabled front of three bays having a four-centred arched doorway and pointed-arched windows.

HORNTON

(60) Former PRIMITIVE METHODIST (SP 393451). Built 1836 behind cottage to left of 1884 chapel, latterly a youth club but now disused. Stone and slate with round-arched doorway and window above in gabled front; two windows in side wall with keystones to lintels and remains of leaded glazing in large panes.

KINGHAM

(61) WESLEYAN (SP 262241). Rubble and slate, with gabled ends, two round-arched windows in the side walls and one above the N entrance. Refitted c.1872 but probably built in the early 19th century.

LANGFORD

(62) CONGREGATIONAL (SP 247029). Services began c.1840 in a barn; the first chapel was built alongside in 1850 and rebuilt in 1884. The barn, which remains in use as a Sunday-school, was partly refaced c.1853 and has a stone gabled front with pointed-arched windows; it is linked to the chapel by a low range of building perhaps also converted from farm use.

Summers (1905) 239–41.

(63) PRIMITIVE METHODIST (SP 248027). Dated 1849, 'Ground Kindly Given by Mr J.K. Tombs'.

LAUNTON

(64) CONGREGATIONAL (SP 610225). Rubble with ashlar dressings and slate roof, front with pineapple finials and large tablet inscribed 'BETHEL/1850'. Original benches with panelled backs and shaped arm-rests.

LEAFIELD

(65) BAPTIST (SP 314153). Rubble with ashlar dressings and hipped slate roof. Three-bay front closely resembling (25) above. Perhaps built as a Congregational chapel, opened 1838.

Summers (1905) 299.

LEW

(66) Former CONGREGATIONAL (SP 321059). Built 1840. Pointed-arched entrance, quatrefoil tablet in gable above.

(64) LAUNTON. Congregational chapel.

(65) LEAFIELD. Baptist chapel.

LITTLE TEW

(67) BAPTIST (SP 385284). Dated 1871. Cusped windows under square labels and unusual crow-stepped gable with finial.

LOWER HEYFORD

(68) Former WESLEYAN, Caulcott (SP 509243). Built 1841, closed 1955 and converted to garage.

MILTON

(69) Former PRESBYTERIAN (SP 449351). The house of Samuel Cox was licensed for Presbyterian use in 1672 and a meeting-house subsequently provided which is described in a trust deed of 1708 as standing 'in the Backside or Close belonging to a Messuage or tenement of the said Samuel Cox the elder' then occupied by his son Simon. The meeting-house, evidently in use for some years previously but perhaps erected for this purpose, was 'about Three Bayes' in length and had a thatched roof. After the demise of the then Unitarian congregation c.1842, which enjoyed a joint pastorate with Bloxham (q.v.), the meeting-

house was used *c*.1850–7 as a chapel-of-ease for Adderbury prior to the erection of the present parish church and subsequently as cottages. Amherst Tyssen writing in 1920 says that 'the building . . . was demolished a few years ago'. A fragment of rubble walling on the W side of Chapel Lane, just N of Chapel Cottage, has been identified as the remains of this building. This now forms part of a row of garages of which the N wall, bounded by larger quoins, survives for its entire length (23½ft externally) and portions of the E and W walls also remain. Some internal wall-plaster is still visible in the NW corner and the lower part of a blocked window with splayed and plastered jambs is to be seen internally on the W wall.

UHST II, pt 2 (1920) 9–32.

MILTON-UNDER-WYCHWOOD

(70) BAPTIST (SP 263180). A chapel opened in 1808 was reported in 1839 to be in a dangerous state. It was replaced in the same year by the present building at a reported cost of £372. 9s. 6½d. The front wall is of ashlar in three bays. The interior has a rear gallery; the pews were renewed in the late 19th century. *Monument*: in chapel, Rev. John 'Hiorns' or Hirons, first pastor, 1844, and Susannah his wife, 1844.

Davidson, G.W., *A Brief History of the Baptist Church, Milton, Oxfordshire* [*c*.1905].

(71) STRICT BAPTIST (SP 264182). 'Zoar Chapel' was built in 1841. The entrance is covered by a modern porch, a stone above is pierced with ventilating holes to form the date 1883, presumably that of a major refurbishing.

Oliver (1968) 116.

(72) Former WESLEYAN (SP 264181). The former 'Wesleyan Mission Room' is a low building of stone and slate built *c*.1860.

In the gable facing the road is a small niche carved below with the denominational name and containing a fragment of mediaeval carving in wood representing an ecclesiastic playing a flute, perhaps removed from the parish church when rebuilt in 1854 (see p. 186).

MINSTER LOVELL

(73) Former PRIMITIVE METHODIST, Charterville (SP 313101). Dated 1892 or 1898. Gate with scrolled supports and railings in front of chapel, wrought-iron, 18th-century, reset.

MOLLINGTON

(74) Former PRIMITIVE METHODIST (SP 440474). Built 1845 and refronted *c*.1860, closed 1947 and subsequently used by Brethren, now in secular occupation. Red brick and slate with two windows in E and W sides, the foremost windows heightened, and entrance at S end of W side: The S front, block-bonded to the sides, has dressings of dark brick with vitrified headers comprising terminal pilasters, entablature and raking cornices to the gable, and two windows with round-arched heads in glazed headers. Part of the structure of a S gallery remains.

NETTLEBED

(75) Former CONGREGATIONAL (SU 703869). Tablet in S gable 'Erected 1838'; altered after 1968 on conversion to house.

Summers (1905) 124–5.

OXFORD

(76) BAPTIST, New Road (SP 512062). A Baptist church was in existence by 1656 in which year it sent messengers to the Abingdon Association. The cause fell into decay in the early 18th cen-

(76) OXFORD. Baptist chapel.

tury and when, in 1715, the Baptist and Presbyterian meeting-houses were severely damaged by rioters the two societies united and built a new meeting-house in New Road *c*.1721. The church was reorganized in 1780 without restriction on baptismal beliefs, but a secession of paedobaptists in 1830 left the other party in the majority.

The present chapel dates from a rebuilding of 1798 of which only parts of the side walls now remain. This was a square building of rubble with a hipped roof surmounted by an octagonal lantern. The front had two doorways alternating with three circular windows and two larger circular or oval windows above. In 1819 the chapel was enlarged to the S and the present front built; this is of ashlar in three bays with a central pedimented porch, having paired Roman Doric columns, between small round-arched windows and rusticated corner pilasters; the upper stage has a central bay with Ionic columns and a wide stilted lunette window, round-arched niches to the side bays, and corner pilasters. The side walls were raised in brickwork and the building re-roofed and refitted *c*.1896. (Interior reported entirely altered 1980)

Fittings – *Monuments*: in chapel (1) Samuel Steane, 1832, and Emma his widow, 1840; (2) John Bartlett, 1822, Jane his widow, 1825, and their children; (3) Thomas Pasco, 1806; (4) Jesse Elliston, 1853; (5) Rev. James Hinton, 1823.

New Road Baptist Church, Oxford... Tercentenary Booklet (1953): Summers (1905) 246–50.

(77) Former BAPTIST, The Croft, Headington (SP 544074). The chapel, built *c*.1835 and superseded *c*.1900 by the present Baptist

chapel in Old High Street, may have been interdenominational in origin. It has walls of squared stone with a gabled S front of three bays. The windows are small and of two four-centred arched lights; the entrance is similarly arched and has a quatrefoil above. Under conversion to cottage, 1977.

(78) Former METHODIST, New Inn Hall Street (SP 51200625). Houses, nos. 32 and 34, were built or converted in the late 18th century for use as a Methodist preaching-house and a modern tablet records visits by John Wesley on 14 July 1783 and later. It was superseded by a new Wesleyan chapel, built in 1818 to designs by William Jenkins on a site further N on the opposite side of the road but now demolished, and again in 1878 by the present Gothic chapel in the same street, by Charles Bell.

The former preaching-house has rubble walls and a hipped tiled roof. The W front is of two stories with a wide doorway near the S end. (For mediaeval vaulting incorporated in N wall see RCHM *City of Oxford* (1939), mon. 124.)

Dolbey (1964) 173: Oxley, J.E., *A History of Wesley Memorial Church, Oxford, 1818–1968* (1967–8).

(79) Former WESLEYAN. Rose Hill, Cowley (SP 535039). Built 1835 by Henry Leake of Iffley but transferred to United Methodist Free Church in 1860. Widened, porch built and round arches added to windows in 20th century. *Monument*: in burial ground, John Leonard, 1846, *et al.*, headstone reset.

VCH *Oxfordshire* V (1957) 94.

(80) SALVATION ARMY, Castle Street (SP 511061). Red brick with S front in two stories, end bays treated as towers with

(80) OXFORD. Salvation Army Citadel.

battlements and tall roofs with iron cresting. Dated 1888, Com. Sherwood, architect. Windows have opaque glass with yellow bands and red squares at intersections. (Demolished since 1970)

PIDDINGTON

(81) CONGREGATIONAL (SP 641174). Built 1848. Three-bay gabled front; contemporary iron railings.

RAMSDEN

(82) Former WESLEYAN (SP 355152). Built 1832. Gabled front with round-arched doorway and two segmental-arched upper windows.

ROLLRIGHT

(83) EBENEZER CHAPEL (SP 323311), formerly Baptist but now in domestic use, is dated 1833. Coursed stone walls with two tall windows and doorway to left in front, all with flat-arched heads. Cottages adjoin at each end.

(84) BETHEL CHAPEL (SP 324311), built 1838, probably by seceders from 'Ebenezer' and of similar materials, has an entrance in the exposed gable wall, two windows at the front and one at the back. Now used for storage.

ROTHERFIELD PEPPARD

(85) CONGREGATIONAL (SU 708809). The chapel, now concealed by the manse and later buildings to E and W, was opened in 1796 and paid for by Peter French, one of the trustees of Castle Street Chapel, Reading. It has brick walls and a hipped tiled roof; the later roofs are slated. The entrance is at the E side but was perhaps formerly at the S before the erection of the manse. A window in the W wall at mid height has been blocked and replaced in the early 19th century by two windows to the south. There are two windows of two lights in the N wall. An aisle was added to the W in the early 19th century and a British school-room was built to the E in the late 19th century, possibly replacing a second aisle. The interior (originally $33\frac{3}{4}$ft by $19\frac{3}{4}$ft) has a gallery at the S end. Colonnades of three timber columns with moulded caps and bases divide the building. *Monument*: in W aisle, Rev. Joseph Walker, 1828, pastor upwards of 30 years, Elizabeth his wife, 1816, and their children Rev. Joseph Walker,

Independent pastor at Bracknell, 1811, William, 1807, Henry, 1805, and Mary Ann Saunders, 1849, signed Wheeler, Reading.
Summers (1905) 152–6.

SALFORD

(86) WESLEYAN (SP 288280). Small square building of rubble and slate with later porch; opened 1848.

SHENINGTON

(87) Former CHAPEL (SP 376428). Built *c*.1817 by Independents but subsequently occupied by Primitive Methodists. Closed after 1962 and entirely altered on conversion to a house.

SHILTON

(88) BAPTIST (SP 266084). Originally a small barn with cart entrance in side wall facing lane. Church formed 1830; pointed-arched windows and pedimented doorway of later 19th century.

SHIPTON-ON-CHERWELL AND THRUPP

(89) Former BAPTIST, Thrupp (SP 483159). Rubble and slate, gabled to NW with porch and large blocked window with tablet in infilling dated 1876. Round-arched windows in side walls with traces of earlier openings. Early 19th-century with contemporary cottages to SE, original use uncertain. (Chapel derelict 1970)

SHUTFORD

(90) Former FRIENDS (SP 386404). Coursed stone walls and a tiled roof; built as a meeting-house in the late 17th century and converted to a cottage *c*.1840.

The S front has at the centre a window with flat-arched head and wood frame of two lights, and a small later dormer above; the original doorway to the right has a flat-arched head and contemporary moulded oak frame and plank door; a cottage door-

Former Friends'
Meeting-house
SHUTFORD
Oxfordshire

way at the opposite end of this wall replaces a window. The E and W walls are gabled and surmounted by small brick chimney-stacks of recent date; there is a single window centrally to ground and first floors at each end. The N wall is blank.

The interior (18¼ft by 33¼ft) was divided by two partitions with shutters to form narrow ground-floor rooms at the E and W ends, the E room having a segmental-arched fireplace in the NW corner and an original staircase with flat balusters and newel with ball finial in the SE corner giving access to a gallery of which the plain slatted balustraded front remains in an upper partition. A similar gallery appears to have existed at the W end; the area between was floored over in the 19th century.

(91) Former WESLEYAN (SP 385403). Opened 1837, much altered.

SIBFORD GOWER

(92) FRIENDS (SP 352378). A small meeting-house of 1678–81 was rebuilt in 1864 to meet an increased demand resulting from

the proximity of the Friends' school at Sibford Ferris. Stone and slate with gabled S front between lower cloak-room wings. Single meeting-room with lobby to S and stand against N wall. Blocked doorway in W wall and trace of partition at S end of room indicate minor alterations.

(93) WESLEYAN (SP 352379). Brick and slate, opened 1827. *Monuments*: in front of chapel (1) Thomas Bloxham, 1839; (2) Sarah, wife of William Matthews, 1848, and their children Mary Ann, and William; (3) John Woodfield, 1843, and Maria his wife, 1839.

SOUTH NEWINGTON

(94) Former FRIENDS (SP 407331). The meeting-house built in 1692, now used as a village hall, has walls of squared ironstone rubble, the roof is covered with stone slates. The S front has a central entrance covered by a porch built in 1927; a tablet above with the inscription 'DOMVS HÆC/QVÆ ÆDIFICERET/ ANNO:DOM:/.1692:RC:*JB*'. A small dormer window near the W end lights one end of a gallery. The E and W walls are gabled and the latter has an ashlar chimney-stack at the apex. The interior (29¾ft by 18¼ft) has a W gallery, probably inserted in the later 18th century, and a fireplace below in the NW corner. The

Former FRIENDS' MEETING-HOUSE, SOUTH NEWINGTON

roof is supported by two arched-braced collar trusses. No original fittings remain.

SOUTH STOKE

(95) INDEPENDENT (SU 599834). The chapel, built in 1820 in association with the Countess of Huntingdon's congregation at Goring, has brick walls and a hipped tiled roof. Entrance at E end with gallery window over and two windows in S side. Date 1820 and initials EH on bricks at W end of S wall.

Summers (1905) 110–11.

STANDLAKE

(96) BAPTIST, Brightampton (SP 387034). Rubble and slate with pointed-arched windows and three-bay gabled front; built 1832 for a section of the church at Cote. (Now closed.)

Stanley [c.1935] 191–2.

STEEPLE BARTON

(97) Former WESLEYAN, Middle Barton (SP 435259), on E side of Worton Road. Rubble with half-hipped slate roof. Built c.1835, closed before 1939 and much altered to a cottage.

STOKE ROW

(98) INDEPENDENT (SU 684840). Brick on flint footings with hipped slate roof. Three-bay S front with later gabled porch; two windows in E and W sides. *Inscriptions*: on bricks in side walls, date of erection, 1815, and initials. *Monument*: in chapel on E wall, John Olding Alanson, 1831, 'Who in the hands of GOD was a willing and efficient Instrument in the erection of this Chapel'.

STONESFIELD

(99) Former WESLEYAN (SP 391171). Stone walls and half-hipped roof covered with Stonesfield slates; porch added 1907, tablet above inscribed 'WESLEYAN CHAPEL 1827'. Superseded 1867 by present chapel 100 yards north-east.

TACKLEY

(100) WESLEYAN, Lower Hades Road (SP 478206). Dated 1853. Probably the conversion of a small early 19th-century barn.

THAME

(101) BAPTIST, Park Street (SP 710056). Dated 1865.
Baines, A.H.J., *The Baptists of Thame* [c.1965].

(102) CONGREGATIONAL, High Street (SP 708057). Gabled front of rubble with brick sides, by W.F. Poulton of Reading, 1871. Organ in small rounded apse behind pulpit; schoolrooms below. (URC)

    CYB (1872) 414.

(103) WESLEYAN, High Street (SP 707058). Wesleyans met from 1778 to 1853 in the former Presbyterian meeting-house in Sun Yard, originally registered in 1728. The present chapel of 1876, replacing one of 1853 which was destroyed by fire, has a gabled stone front with three graduated lancet windows and octagonal corner pinnacles. (Converted to secular use *c.*1977 and congregation united with (102) above)

WATLINGTON

(104) WESLEYAN (SU 691945). Dated 1812. W front in Flemish bond with glazed headers and cast-iron gable ornaments. Original gallery around three sides, seating later.

WEST ADDERBURY

(105) Former INDEPENDENT (SP 468355). Pedimented ashlar front with circular tablet dated 1829. Doorway widened on conversion to industrial use.

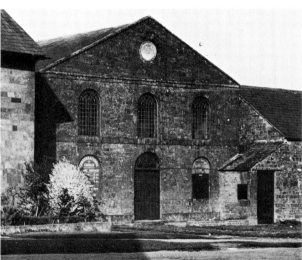

(106) Former FRIENDS (SP 465354). The meeting-house, now a store for adjacent public cemetery, was built in 1675 by Bray Doyley or D'Oyly of Adderbury, a prominent Quaker. It has walls of coursed rubble and the roof, formerly covered with stone slates, is now tiled. The S front has a wide central entrance

(106) WEST ADDERBURY. Former Friends' meeting-house. (Chimney stack dated 1675).

between two windows with wooden frames of three lights and leaded glazing. Above the entrance is a small gabled dormer. The E and W walls are gabled and have shaped kneelers and parapets; at the W end is an ashlar chimney-stack with a panel on the S face bearing the date 1675. There is a wide upper window of three lights in the W wall, a similar window to the lower floor at the E end, and a smaller window above. A window appears to have formerly existed centrally in the N wall.

The interior (19ft by 30¾ft) has deep galleries with plain balustraded fronts around the E, S and W sides, possibly the extension of a gallery or upper room at the W end only, where one roof truss remains closed above collar level. The stand against the N wall dates from the 18th century.

A smaller meeting-house, demolished c.1955, stood to the S and had rubble walls and a thatched roof; it was built in the early 18th century for women's meetings and later became a cottage.

The burial-ground to the E contains uniform headstones of 19th century and later, also, fixed to S boundary wall, four cast-iron monuments with pointed-arched heads, of 1855–79.

Arnold (1960) 101–3.

WESTON-ON-THE-GREEN

(107) WESLEYAN, North Lane (SP 532189). Dated 1838.

WHEATLEY

(108) BRETHREN (SP 594058). An early 19th-century granary with rubble walls lined in brickwork and gabled ends with shaped kneelers. Converted by partial removal of upper floor leaving a gallery at one end.

(109) CONGREGATIONAL (SP 598056). A late 18th-century barn or outbuilding associated with an adjacent tannery was con-

verted to a meeting-house about 1842 and the front wall rebuilt. The walls are of rubble and the roof is tiled. The gabled NE front has three lancet windows and a former central entrance now replaced by a gabled SE porch. Traces of an earlier wide cart-entrance with timber lintel remain in the NW wall. (URC)

Summers (1905) 265–8.

WIGGINGTON

(110) Former BAPTIST (SP 390331). Coursed ironstone walls, ashlar front, and roof re-covered in tiles; three-bay front with keystones to lintels and formerly external shutters to the windows. Built c.1835.

WITNEY

(111) Former PRESBYTERIAN, Meeting-house Lane (SP 355097). A Presbyterian society appears to have been in existence in Witney by 1672 in which year Francis Hubert (or Hubbard), ejected vicar of Winterbourne Monkton, licensed his house for meetings. The present building, erected in 1712 during the ministry of Samuel Mather, grandson of the Puritan divine Richard Mather of Toxteth Chapel, Liverpool, continued to serve the society until 1828 when a new chapel was built in High Street (see below). The congregation suffered from various divisions in the late 18th century due in part to the presence of a considerable Baptist element, but became more firmly established as a Congregational cause in the early 19th century. After 1828 the meeting-house was used for Sunday-school and other church purposes; it now serves as a Scout hall.

The meeting-house, said to have been paid for out of the private fortune of Samuel Mather's wife, a Townsend of Staple Hall, is a rectangular building with tall rubble walls and a tiled roof. The N and S ends are gabled, each having a tall upper window and at the S end next to the lane is a wide central doorway with an early 18th-century wood frame. The W wall, concealed from view by an adjoining late 19th-century brick building, faces towards the premises of the Batt School; it has a pair of windows set close together which formerly flanked a central pulpit and two windows towards the ends; that to the S is blocked, the others have timber lintels and original wooden cross-frames. The E wall has two similar windows more widely spaced.

Monuments: reported 1951 as internal were (1) Thomas Howell, 1780; (2) Richard Witts, 1755, Jane his widow, 1770, and Richard their son, 1828; (3) James Marriott, 1803. The last was (1969) loose in the 1828 chapel.

Summers (1905) 268–75.

(112) CONGREGATIONAL, High Street (SP 355098). Built in 1828 at the expense of William Townsend, of the same family as the wife of Samuel Mather whose money had paid for the earlier

building. The walls are of squared stone. The E front is of ashlar; the principal windows, of two lights with uncusped tracery, are set in projecting panels surmounted by false parapets. Above the entrance is a circular window with quatrefoil tracery and in the gable is a tablet with the inscription 'ERECTED/BY/WILLIAM TOWNSEND/OF/HOLBORN, LONDON/A.D. MDCCCXXVIII' with a small shield-of-arms below. The interior has a flat plaster ceiling with moulded cornice, central plaster ceiling-rose and four ventilating grilles with Gothic tracery. A gallery at the E end has a panelled front supported by cast-iron columns.

Fittings – *Bootscrapers*: pair, at front entrance, cast iron, 1828. *Monuments*: in chapel on N wall (1) Mary (Roffey) wife of Rev. Robert Tozer, 1837; on S wall (2) Rev. Robert Tozer, 18 years

minister, 1855. *Organ*: small, with wooden case, front of five panels with crocketed central arch, pinnacled corners and dummy pipes, mid 19th-century. *Pulpit*: original front of three panelled sides reduced in height and set on late 19th-century plat-

Congregational Chapel, WITNEY

Oxfordshire

5   0   5   10   15 Feet

N

Gallery over

C.F.S.

form. *Railings*: in front of chapel, wrought-iron, rising in centre to double gates with tall standards and scrolled overthrow, 1828. (Chapel demolished *c*.1970–2 and replaced by a supermarket)

Summers (1905) 268–75.

(113) Former FRIENDS, Wood Green Hill (SP 360104). A meeting-house of 1676 was replaced in 1712 by the present building, but this was not registered until January 1745/6. It was enlarged to the NE in the late 18th century and a wing added to the NW a century later. The walls are of rubble and the roof is covered with stone slates. The original structure has been much altered. The SW wall is gabled and has one blocked lower window and another above with a large timber lintel surviving from a previous window. The SE wall, facing the burial-ground, has two segmental-arched windows of the late 18th century and

SE wall.

the remains of former openings including a wide doorway near the SW end and a window alongside with external timber lintel. The NE extension has at the front a segmental-arched doorway with rusticated brick arch and jambs and double doors and at the back a corresponding pair of doors with vertical panelling.

The interior (41ft by 18ft) has a narrow NE gallery with an original fireplace. The walls have a panelled dado which rises at the SW end behind the site of the stand; a false wall behind the stand and a flat canopy above probably date from *c*.1800. The NE extension comprises a wide stone-paved entrance-passage with minor rooms on the ground floor and a single room above; the staircase has a straight moulded string of the late 18th century and a ball finial to the lower newel. The roof is supported by two trusses with exposed tie-beams and two collars; the plaster ceiling has been inserted. (In use 1969 as a hall, converted to residential use *c*.1980)

Inscriptions: (1) inside SW gable, on plaster surface of original window lintel, 'Richard May'; (2) on glazing quarry in SW window of upper room at NE end 'Wm Mills glazier Witney 1786'.

(114) WESLEYAN, High Street (SP 357099). Rubble walls and slated roof, in Gothic style by J. Wilson of Bath, 1850, replacing a chapel of 1800. Narrow gabled entrance bay facing street with tall window of four lights and cusped tracery in a two-centred head. A decorative bell-cote and elaborate pinnacles have been removed. Five lancet windows in low side walls. Galleried interior. *Bootscrapers*: at entrance, pair, cast-iron, double arms bracketed to single standard.

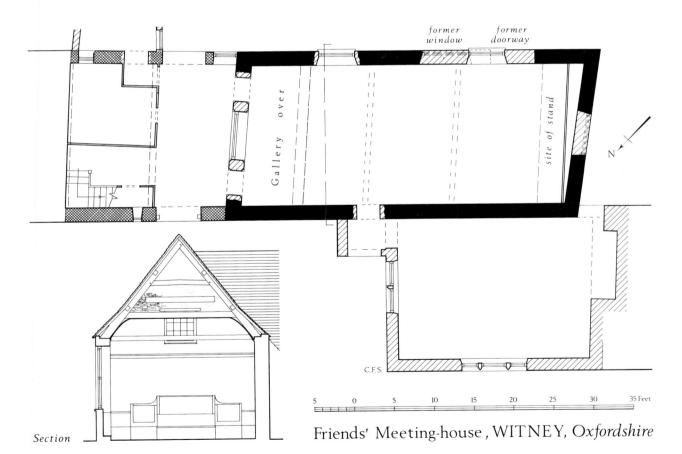

Section

Friends' Meeting-house, WITNEY, *Oxfordshire*

(115) WESLEYAN, Newland (SP 363101). Gabled front with upper window; concealed behind other buildings. Opened 1828.

WOODSTOCK

(116) BAPTIST, High Street (SP 445167). Rendered front of three bays with pediment, round-arched doorway and windows with marginal lights. Built early 19th century for a church formed c.1825–7.

WROXTON

(117) WESLEYAN, Balscote (SP 391419). Small chapel with walls of squared ironstone and slated roof; dated 1850.

(118) Former WESLEYAN, Wroxton (SP 413418), behind 'Sundial Farmhouse'. Built c.1820, with walls of squared stone and a slate roof. Two windows in W front with entrance near S end replaced by garage doors. Site of pulpit at N end with painted inscription on wall and traces of gallery opposite. Present chapel 250 yards W dated 1935.

(72) MILTON-UNDER-WYCHWOOD: Former Wesleyan Mission Room. Mediaeval carving.